italian for homebuyers

italian for homebuyers

peter macbride

and giulia gigliotti

The publisher has used its best endeavours to ensure that the URLs referred to in this book are correct and active at the time of going to press. However, the publisher and the author have no responsibilities for the websites and can make no guarantee that a site will remain live or that the content will remain relevant, decent or appropriate.

For UK order enquiries: please contact Bookpoint Ltd, 130 Milton Park, Abingdon, Oxon OX14 4SB. Telephone: +44 (0)1235 827720. Fax: +44 (0)1235 400454. Lines are open 09.00–17.00, Monday to Saturday, with a 24-hour message answering service. Details about our titles and how to order are available at www.teachyourself.co.uk.

Long renowned as the authoritative source for self-guided learning – with more than 50 million copies sold worldwide – the **teach yourself** series includes over 500 titles in the fields of languages, crafts, hobbies, business, computing and education.

British Library Cataloguing in Publication Data.
A catalogue record for this title is available from The British Library.

Library of Congress Catalog Number: on file.

First published in UK 2005 by Hodder Education, 338 Euston Road, London, NW1 3BH. This edition published 2007.

The **teach yourself** name is a registered trade mark of Hodder Headline Ltd.

Computer hardware and software brand names mentioned in this book are protected by their respective trademarks and are acknowledged.

Typeset by MacDesign, Southampton

Printed in Great Britain for Hodder Education, an Hachette Livre UK Company, 338 Euston Road, London NW1 3BH by Cox & Wyman Ltd, Reading, Berkshire.

Hodder Headline's policy is to use papers that are natural, renewable and recyclable products and made from wood grown in sustainable forests. The logging and manufacturing processes are expected to conform to the environmental regulations of the country of origin.

Impression number   10 9 8 7 6 5 4 3 2 1

Year   2011 2010 2009 2008 2007

contents

preface

The thought behind this book is a simple one. If you want to buy a house in Italy, it helps if you know the words. This isn't the same as being able to speak Italian – even with a degree in Italian, you may not know your *contratto di compravendita* (contract of sale) from your *abbaino* (dormer window). No, you don't actually have to be able to speak Italian – though it helps no end if you do – but if you know the words that describe houses and their various components, and the words that are involved in the sale process, then you will be better equipped for finding, buying and settling into your Italian home.

Italian for homebuyers covers nearly 1000 of the most useful words for home buyers and home owners, but this book is not a dictionary. A translation alone is sometimes not enough. It doesn't get you much further to know that *notaio* translates to 'notary', or that *spagnoletta* means 'shutter fastener'. You need to know what the *notaio*'s role is and how it affects you, and what a *spagnoletta* looks like. The words are given here in the context of the buying process or of different aspects of the house. Where it will help, we've tried to explain the concepts behind the words or to give an illustration.

Thanks are due to all who helped in the production of this book, especially Tony Jones of Art Construction, Sue Hart and Ginny Catmur of Hodder and Stoughton, Mike Hayes of Homes Overseas, Catherine McGregor, our copy-editor, and Jake MacBride, our UK building consultant. We would also like to thank our friends and neighbours in France and Italy.

Peter MacBride and Giulia Gigliotti

The CD

The CD that accompanies this book is designed to be used along-side Chapter 10, *Un'ora di italiano – an hour of Italian*. There are 20 tracks:

Track 1 is a very brief introduction to the Italian language, covering pronunciation, how to greet people, ask questions and understand simple replies.

The remaining tracks all give practice in speaking and listening to some of the most important or useful words in each chapter. It should take between 5 and 15 minutes to complete each one – work through a track before going out to tackle a job and you will be better prepared to deal with the *agenti* and the *operai*.

Track 2 links to Chapter 1, *La ricerca – the search*

Track 3 links to Chapter 2, *La vendita – the sale*

Track 4 links to Chapter 3, *I lavori – building work*

Tracks 5–7 link to Chapter 4, *La struttura – the structure*

Track 5: *Talking to il muratore – the builder*

Track 6: *Finding tools and materials at the negozio di Fai-da-Te – the DIY store*

Track 7: *Talking to il falegname – the roof carpenter – and il copritetto – the roofer*

Tracks 8–10 link to Chapter 5, *Le opere in legno – woodwork*

Track 8: *Talking to il carpentiere – the joiner*

Track 9: *Finding materials at the negozio di Fai-da-Te*

Track 10: *Finding tools at the negozio di Fai-da-Te*

Tracks 11–13 link to Chapter 6, *L'impianto idraulico – plumbing*

Track 11: *Talking to l'idraulico – the plumber*

Track 12: *Shopping for bathroom and kitchen equipment*

Track 13: *Finding tools at the negozio di Fai-da-Te*

The voices on the CD are those of Lara Parmiani and Stuart Nurse.

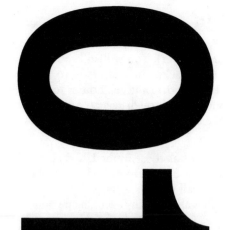

01

la ricerca –
the search

Almost the same...

There was a time when most houses were sold directly by the owner, working with a *notaio* (lawyer). You will still sometimes see hand-written *in vendita* signs tacked to shutters or to a post in the garden, and *notaios* still advertise and sell houses for their clients, but most houses now are sold through *agenzie immobiliari* (estate agents). This can make the search simpler for us overseas buyers.

Italian agents are almost the same as those in the UK. The most visible difference is that they are tight-fisted with their information sheets – you can't call them handouts if they aren't handed out! In the UK, you can walk in to any agent, help yourself to sheets on as many houses as you like, and take them away to study at your leisure. In a typical Italian agency you see a selection of sheets on display in the window, and perhaps inside. When you enter, you will be offered a loose-leaf file to browse through at a desk. The sheets tend to have less information than those of UK agents, but what the *agenzie immobiliari* don't put on the sheets, they keep in their notes and in their heads. The staff usually know their properties and can talk intelligently about them. If you find any that interest you, they will arrange a visit. (And if you insist, they'll make you a black and white photocopy of the sheet!)

But before we get into an agent's office, we have to find one! Let's start the search.

Define your search

Where do you want to buy a house? In which region? In a town, a village or in the countryside? What sort and size of house do you want? How much garden? How much work do you want to have to do on it? Are you looking for a ruin to rebuild, an old house to restore, one that needs a little light redecorating, or a new build? These are questions that only you can answer – this checklist may help you to define your ideal house.

> **If you don't know where you want to be, or what sort of house, spend more time exploring Italy, renting different types of houses in different areas, then start looking.**

Ideal house checklist

Location: Region or province? ....

Town, village or countryside? ....

Is the view important? ....

Max distance from airport ....

Max distance from shops ....

Max distance from cafés/restaurants ....

Max distance from beach/swimming/etc.

Max distance from children's play facilities ....

Size: Number of bedrooms ....

Other rooms ....

Minimum total floorspace (1) ....

Outside: Swimming pool? (Y/N).....................................

Garage/parking needed? (Y/N) ....

Minimum garden/land area................................

Condition: New build, or an existing house? (2) ....

Ruin/renovation/redecoration/ready? (3) ....

What furniture/fittings are present? ....

Budget: How much money is available? ....

How much time do you have (4) ....

(1) The size of a house is normally expressed in total floor area. A cottage or small terraced house is around 50m², 100m² is equivalent to a typical new British semi, 200m² is the size of an older 5-bed detached house in the UK.

(2) Notaio's fees and taxes will add between10% and 20% to the cost of the property (see page 42).

(3) If you plan to rebuild or restore, you must have some idea of the cost of building work and be prepared to deal with the paperwork (see Chapter 3).

(4) The less time you have to work on the house, the more professional services you will have to buy.

The regions of Italy

1	Piedmont	11	Marches
2	Aosta Valley	12	Latium
3	Lombardy	13	Abruzzo
4	Trentino-Alto Adig	14	Molise
5	Veneto	15	Campania
6	Friuli-Venezia Giulia	16	Apulia
7	Liguria Genoa	17	Basilicata
8	Emilia-Romagna	18	Calabria
9	Tuscany	19	Sicily
10	Umbria	20	Sardinia

Searching through the Web

Get online before you leave home and give yourself a head start. You may be able to find your Italian house through the Web, but even if you don't find a specific one, you will find the more active agents and get a good idea of the prices in an area.

If you miss out the Web search, you will spend the first days of your visit hunting through the *Pagine Gialle* (Yellow Pages) or the town itself looking for the *agenzie immobiliari*.

The sites fall into three main types: those of UK-based agents, those of nation-wide Italian estate agents, and those of local Italian agents.

UK-based property sites

As well as advertising houses, these offer varying levels of help with buying and settling in, e.g. arranging mortgages, translating legal documents, linking with English-speaking craftsmen. The main limitation, of course, is that they only have a tiny proportion of the houses on the market.

Here are some UK-based sites that you may find useful:

- *The Move Channel* advertises properties for agents across Italy (and many other countries), giving brief details and passing on requests for further information to the agents. You can search the site freely, though if you want to find out more about any given property must register before they will connect you with the agents. They don't have huge selection of properties, but if you can find one in the right place, that's more or less what you are looking for, then its agent could be a good initial contact. The site also has good sets of links to sites offering financial, legal and other services for people buying overseas. Find them at: **http://www.themovechannel.com** and click the Italian flag.

- *Sunshine Estates* is another international site, but with an excellent choice of Italian properties – at the time of writing they were advertising over 1200 properties, from €12,000 to €25million. The search facility is easy to use, and responds very quickly. Find them at **www.sunshineestates.net**, and select Italy in the Search form.

The Move Channel is a good source of help and advice as well as a useful place to start your search.

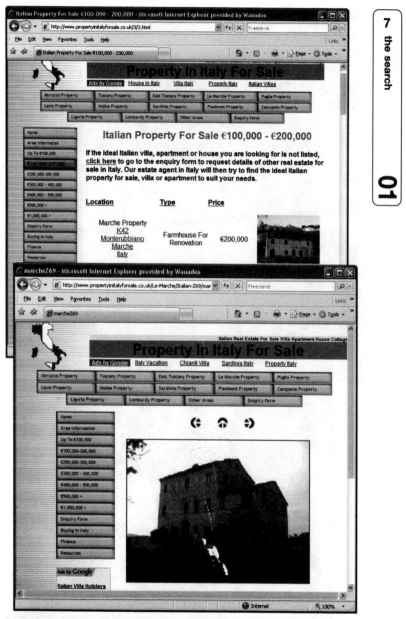

Property in Italy for Sale has a huge selection of houses, apartments and other properties throughout Italy.

Properties around Italy have lots on offer, with detailed information and photographs for each property.

- **Properties around Italy** are specialists in Italian properties, and have a good selection on offer, with plenty of details on each one. As well as advertising, the company also offers maintenance and restoration services, and can help with mortgages, tax and legal aspects of house-buying in Italy. They are at **www.propertiesarounditaly.com**

- **Tuscany real estate** focus in 'Chiantishire' – the Italian region that has long been the most popular deal with UK buyers. At the time of writing they had an excellent range, from €30,000 restoration projects, up to wonderful historical villas at €3million. The Tuscany Guide at their site is very informative, and they have some good links to other useful sites. Find them at **www.tuscanyrealestate.co.uk**

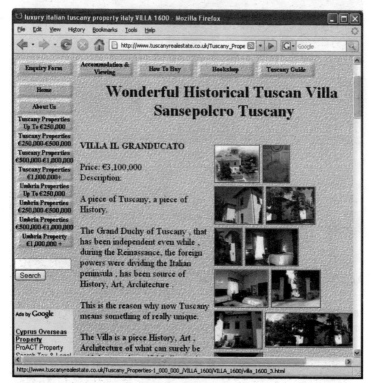

Ah, dream on! But the **Tuscany Real Estate** site also carries notices for many properties at prices more of us can afford, and some interesting restoration projects for the more adventurous.

- **Tuscany villas** specialises in rural villas and farmhouses and village houses in Tuscany. If that's where you want to buy, this site is well worth a visit. They have good sets of photos and plenty of information about most of their properties. Find them at **www.tuscanvillas.net**

And here's a restoration project at **Tuscan Villas** – there's a bit of work to do, but look at the views and that fireplace! And you've got your own private chapel – all for €90,000.

- **Casambiente** are based in Italy, but cater mainly for English-speaking clients. They have a good selection of houses in Umbria, and offer construction and restoration services, as well as advice and help with arranging purchases. Visit their site at **www.casambiente.com**

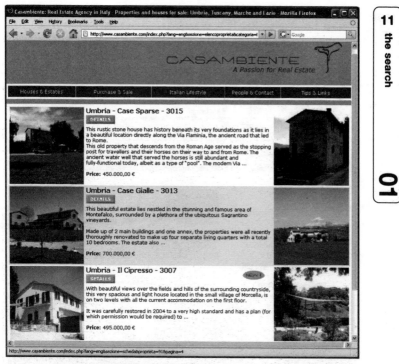

Even if you are not looking for a house in Umbria, **Casambiente**'s web site is worth visiting for its advice on buying properties in Italy.

Le agenzie immobiliari – estate agents

Italy has only a few national *agenzie immobiliari*. Most cover just one or more regions, or are purely local. The larger agents, and an increasing number of the small ones, have web sites, and most sites have a search facility. The searches vary, but tend to follow the same pattern – you will be asked to specify the type of property, price range and the region or province (except at a local agent's site). At some sites, you can pinpoint the location down to the area within a town.

These sites are worth visiting:

> *Systemacasa* handles property all over Italy. Their *ricerca avanzata* (advanced search) page allows you to set very precise specifications for a property – the exact place, a tight price range, the amount of land, the number of rooms, and other

options – even including the type of kitchen. Being too specific can be a mistake. If you narrow the search too much, you may miss a something just a little out of your area or price or size range. Visit them at: **www.systemacasa.it**

The advanced search page at **www.systemacasa.it**. You can specify a place down to the *zona* (local area) but many options can be left at *Qualiasi* (any).

- *Cast.it* is not an agency, but a showplace for agents from all parts of Italy. Theirs is not the easiest site to work through – in fact, their *Ricerca Rapida Immobili* (Quick Search) is one of the most awkward you are ever likely to meet. The map based search is better, especially if you are searching for a house in a particular area – and they do have a lot of properties (around 90,000 at the time of writing). They also have some of the biggest photos around – don't try to view this site on a 800 × 640 screen! Find them at: **www.casa.it**

If you know exactly where you want a house, the standard **Ricerca** routine at **www.casa.it** may lead you to it – though you may find the map-based search facility easier to use.

- *Casaperme* ('house for me') is a small ads site, where house-owners and some smaller estate agents advertise houses. There are two drawbacks to this site. First, there is no search facility, though properties are listed by commune. If you know exactly where you want to look, this is not a problem, just select the region, then the province, then the commune to see what's on offer in that area.Find them at: **www.casaperme.it**

The second catch is that it is a text-only site, and only in Italian. If you're Italian is not good enough to cope with it, here's a solution – go to Google!

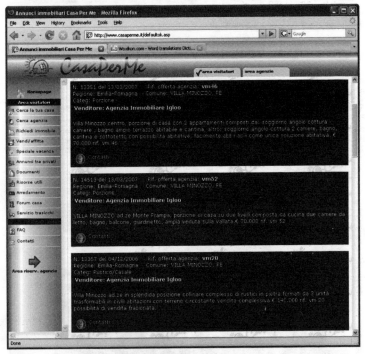

Small ads at **Casaperme**. Start looking by clicking on **Cerca la tua casa**. If you want more details on a property, use the **Contatti** link to e-mail the advertiser.

The Google language tools

Google has language tools that will translate chunks of text, or even whole web pages. The translation won't be exactly perfect, but it should give you a reasonable idea of what the property is like.

Here's how to use it to translate text.

1 Select the text you want to translate, then open the **Edit** menu and select **Copy**.

2 Go to Google at **www. google.com**.

3 Click **Language tools** (on the right of the search box).

4 Click into the **Translate text** area and use **Edit > Paste** to copy in the text.

• If you want to translate a whole page, type its address into the **Translate a Web page** box at step 4.

5 Select **Italian to English** and click [Translate].

The **Google Language Tools** in action – automatic translation has its limitations, as you can see!

Local agenzie immobiliari

Not all *agenzie immobiliari* have web sites, but you can still use the web to find the ones in your area. *Agenzieimmobiliari.com* has lists of estate agents, organised by region and province. Select a region, then a town or area within it, to get a list of names and contact details – and web links, if available. To start looking for local *agenzie immobiliari*, go to **www.agenzieimmobiliari.com**

You can find the estate agents in your area at **AgenzieImmobiliari.com**. Some have adverts at the site (on the right of the regional page), others simply have their details listed (click on a local area for the list).

Of course, you can also use Google to find the local agents. Go to **www.google.com**, and type in *"agenzie immobiliari"* (in double quotes) and the name of the town or province. You will have to do some filtering, but could find some good leads in the resulting links.

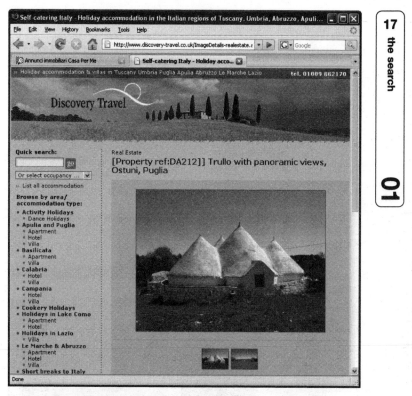

If you want something distinctively different, how about a trullo? These round houses with conical roofs are unique to Puglia. They are quite fashionable, so even a small one, in need of restoration, will cost €60,000 or more. On larger properties, the trullo is often used as a guesthouse and the main house is a villa with more and larger rooms (trullo rooms are typically around 4m in diameter).

Agenzie as searchers

Some UK-based sites and English-speaking agents in areas popular with UK buyers will invite you to send your requirements by e-mail, and will search beyond the properties visible on-line to try to find one to suit you. You will have to pay for this service, either in actual fees or in higher property prices, but may be worth it, especially if you are short of time for searching on the ground.

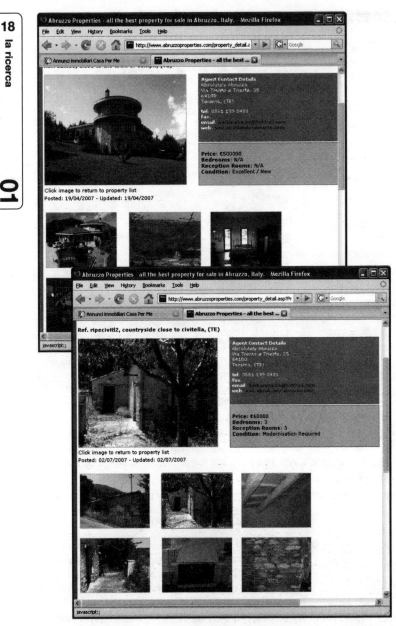

Ready-to-move-into, or a challenge? There are houses to suit all dreams in Italy. We found these two at **www.abruzzoproperties.com**.

Agenzia immobiliare abbreviations

imm.le	immobile	building
apt.	appartamento	flat
uff.	ufficio	office
risc. centr.	riscaldamento centrale	central heating
1° P	primo piano	first floor
risc.	riscaldamento	heating
cam. letto	camere da letto	bedrooms
cam. princ.	camere principali	main rooms
p. terra	piano terra	ground floor
ingr.	ingresso	hall
bg.	bagno	bathroom
sogg.	soggiorno	lounge
sup. ab.	superficie abitabile	floor area

Notaios on-line

The *notaios'* professional organization, *Associazione Italiana Notai*, runs a web site at **http://www.notariato.it**. If you need your own notaio, you can find one through the **Trovare un notaio** link on the top page. (Normally both parties use the same one.) There's lots of advice and information, but only in Italian.

Search on the ground

When you plan your buying trip, allow at least twice as much time as you think is really necessary. Delays can happen, and if everything does goes smoothly, you can relax and treat the rest of your stay as a simple holiday.

If you found potential houses on the Web, contact the *agenzie immobliari* by e-mail or phone to arrange to visit them. Allow plenty of time for each visit. The agencies may have other properties – newly-in or not advertised online – that you may want to see, and each house viewing can take a while.

Use the *Pagine Gialle* (Yellow Pages) directory to find the other local agents and see what they have to offer. And keep an eye out for *in vendita* (for sale) signs outside houses.

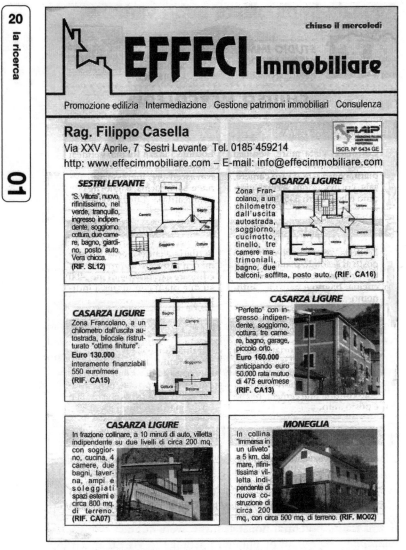

Two pages from a property brochure. In this brochure, each page advertised a selection of properties for a different *agenzie* – and with very different styles. Effeci (above) uses mainly plans to sell apartments, and notice that there is no price given in most of the ads. This may be a reflection of the Italian approach to property prices – a property has an actual price (the one you pay) and a declared price (the one used for tax calculations).

Studio James, in the same brochure, tends to give the views from the properties rather than of them. Well, they do say that the three most important things about a property are location, location, location.

Tecnocasa is an network of agencies, that produces glossy, well illustrated brochures for its members. It also runs a web site (**www.tecnocasa.it**) that you can use to locate the agency in any selected commune. At the time of writing, the site did not carry any property adverts.

Notice that the ads show prices in euro and lira, but the use of commas and decimal points in the number formats can be misleading. Euro 120.000,00 is €120,000 exactly; L. 232.352.400 is 232 million lira (€1 = L1,936).

When you are there, look for the free property brochures outside, or inside, *agenzie* offices. These are one of the main forms of advertising in Italy.

New houses

Italians sometimes prefer new houses to 'second hand' ones – and there is a lot to be said in their favour. New houses have new fully-fitted kitchens and bathrooms; they will be freshly painted and decorated throughout to your specifications; and if you have been involved from an early enough stage, the layout and the number, size and types of rooms may have been customised to your liking.

And, of course, if you start from scratch with a plot of land and your own builder, then the house will be exactly as you want it (if all goes to plan...)

In Italy new houses are subject to *IVA – Imposta sul Valore Aggiunto* (VAT) – currently 19% on luxury homes and 9% on all others. When you are quoted a price for a new house, ask if it includes *IVA*.

Buying for investment?

Some people do buy houses in Italy more as investments than for their own use, hoping for capital growth or rental income or both. If this is your plan, you should be aware of the following: house prices have gone up significantly in recent years, as they have in the UK – and partly fuelled by the UK rises – but at the time of writing (summer 2007) prices seem to be stabilising. There is currently a lot of spare capacity in the holiday rental market – bookings have fallen and more people are offering property – though there are leaseback schemes that offer guarranteed rental income.

There's more on buying property for investment in the appendix (page 181).

Lexicon: la ricerca – the search

acquisto (m)	purchase
agenzia immobiliare (f)	estate agency
agente immobiliare (m)	estate agent
camera (f)	room
casa (f)	house
comprare	to buy
IVA (Imposta sul Valore Aggiunto)	VAT
in vendita	for sale
iniziare (la ricerca)	start (the search at a web site)
lavori da realizzare	work to be done
locale (m)	room
moderna	modern
modificare la ricerca	modify (the search at a web site)
notaio (m)	lawyer, public official
Pagine Gialle	Yellow Pages
precedente	previous
ricerca (f)	search
ricerca avanzata	advanced search
successiva	next
terreno (m)	land (for building)
vano (f)	room

Generi di case – types of houses

bella vista	beautiful view
buone condizioni	good condition
campagna (f)	country
casa (f)	house
casa a schiera	terraced house
casa abbinata	semi-detached
casa borghese	'middle class' – substantial, good quality town house

casa di campagna	country house
casa indipendente	detached house
casa moderna	modern house
casa padronale	manor house
casa realizzata in muratura e legno	half-timbered house (Tudor-style, but probably genuinely old)
casa signorile	gentleman's house
chalet (m)	chalet – wood or wood on stone house in Alpine regions
da restaurare	for restoration (this can mean complete rebuild!)
da rinnovare	for renovation
fienile (m)	barn
mansarda (f)	pigeon loft – often large enough to make a decent room
masseria (f)	farmhouse
mulino (m)	mill
residenza (f)	residence
residenza di campagna (f)	country residence
rete fognaria pubblica	mains drains
rinnovata	renovated
rudere (f)	ruin – expect to knock it down and start from scratch
ristrutturabile	could be converted
sul mare/fiume	by the sea/river
vecchia	old

Vani e attrezzature – rooms and facilities

alimentazione (f)	supply (water, electricity etc.)
alloggio (m)	accomodation
ampliamento (m)	extension
annesso (f)	outbuilding
bagno (m)	bathrooom
camera (f)	room
camera da letto (f)	bedroom

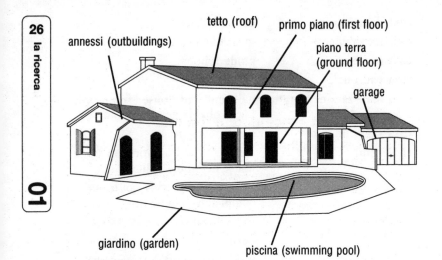

annessi (outbuildings)

tetto (roof)

primo piano (first floor)

piano terra (ground floor)

garage

giardino (garden)

piscina (swimming pool)

cameretta (m)	small room
cantina (f)	cellar
camino (f)	chimney, also refers to fireplace
cucina (f)	kitchen
cucina a vista (f)	open-plan kitchen
fossa biologica (f)	septic tank
garage (m)	garage
giardino (m)	garden
piano terra (m)	ground floor
piscina (f)	swimming pool
primo piano (m)	first floor
proprietà (f)	property
proprietario (m)	owner
ripostiglio (m)	storeroom
ristrutturazione (f) della soffitta	loft conversion
sala da pranzo (f)	dining room
scantinato (m)	basement
soggiorno (m)	living room
solaio/soffitta (m)	attic/loft

studio (m)	study
tariffe pubbliche comprese	service charges included
terreno (m)	grounds
tetto (m)	roof

What's included in the price?

If the house is furnished when you view it, ask very carefully about what will be included in the sale price. It is normal in Italy for the vendor to remove everything that isn't screwed down and quite a lot of what is. The bath, toilet and other sanitaryware are usually left, but the kitchen fittings – including the sink – may be taken, along with garden ornaments, shelves, curtains, light bulbs...

If there is anything in the house that you would like to be there when it becomes yours, tell the agent or the vendor, agree a price and get it written into the initial contract. Most vendors are open to reasonable offers. They're not trying to rip you off – it's just a different way of doing things.

Found it?

You've found a house that's perfect, or as near as perfect as you can get within your budget. What next? There are three key questions that need answering:

- Is the house worth the asking price?
- Is it really within your budget?
- If you intend to adapt, improve or extend the house, will you be allowed to do it?

To get the answers, ask the experts.

Il consulente immobiliare – the valuer

Consulenti immobiliari are called on to value houses not just for purchases, but also as required in divorce settlements and other legal disputes. Their valuation will be based on:

- The prices of other houses sold recently in the same area.

- The state of the house and the cost of essential improvements, e.g. new roof, installation of a septic tank, connection to mains drains, water, gas or electric, and the like.

- The land owned with the property. Old houses, especially in villages, may have a non-adjacent garden or plot of land. The expert will check the *mappa catastale* – the official map that shows the boundaries and ownership of land in the *comune* (the local council area).

- The planning status of the area, as shown in the *comune*'s *PRG* (*piano regolatore generale*) – the town's planning brief. This will tell you what future development may happen in the area around the house, and whether you will be able to adapt it in the way you want to. We will have another look at the PRG in Chapter 3.

- Any rights of way or other encumbrances on the property.

You can find a list of *consulenti immobiliari* at their web site (go to **www.aici-italia.it** and click on the **Siti Dei Soci** on the top page) or by post at:

Associazione Italiana Consulenti e Gestori Immobiliari (AICI)
Viale Nevrino 5
20123 Milano

Do you need a valuation?

You do not have to have a valuation – it is optional. If you are buying a town house or apartment, in good condition and *a basso prezzo* (low price) – and you can still find these places – a valuation is only essential if you are taking out a mortgage, or if you want reassurance about the price.

I preventivi – estimates

If there are limited jobs to do on the house, e.g. a new roof, new bathroom, rewiring, etc. you can ask local tradesmen for a *preventivo* (estimate). You can rely on a *preventivo* to give you an accurate cost of the finished work – as long as you take it up within a few months, and don't redefine the job. If there is more complicated work to be done, approach a *geometra* (surveyor).

They can organise building jobs, and get estimates as well as draw up plans for you. We will come back to the *geometra* and *preventivo* in Chapter 3 when we look at building work.

Lexicon: gli esperti – the experts

geometra (m)	surveyor
consulente immobiliare	valuer
mappa (f) catastale	map of land ownership
preventivo (m)	estimate
PRG (piano regolatore generale)	planning brief

English–Italian quick reference

La ricerca – the search

buy	comprare
estate agency	agenzia immobiliare
for sale	in vendita
house	casa (f)
land (for building)	terreno
modern	moderna(o)
modify (the search)	modificare (la ricerca)
next	successiva
previous	precedente
room	camera (f), locale (m)
search	ricerca (f)
start (the search)	iniziare (la ricerca)
work to be done	lavori da realizzare

Types of houses – generi di case

barn	fienile (m)
beautiful view	bella vista
castle, country residence	residenza di campagna (f)

convert	ristrutturare
country	campagna (f)
good condition	buone condizioni
half-timbered	casa realizzata in muratura e legno
house	casa (f)
mains drains	rete fognaria pubblica (f)
manor house	casa padronale (f)
mill	mulino (m)
old	vecchia(o)
pigeon loft	mansarda (f)
renovate	rinnovare, restaurare
ruin	rudere (m)
semi-detached/terraced	casa abbinata/casa a schiera

Rooms and facilities – vani e attrezzature

accommodation	alloggio (m)
attic	solaio (m)
basement	scantinato (m)
bathroom	bagno (m)
bedroom	camera da letto (f)
cellar	cantina (f)
chimney	camino (m)
dining room	sala da pranzo (f)
extension	ampliamento (m)
fireplace	caminetto (m)
first floor	primo piano (m)
garage	garage (m)
garden	giardino (m)
ground floor	piano terra (m)
grounds	terreno (m)
kitchen	cucina (f)
kitchen, open-plan	cucina a vista
lavatory	gabinetto (m)

living room	soggiorno
loft	granaio (m), soffitta(f)
outbuilding	annesso (f)
owner	proprietario (m)
property	proprietà (f)
roof	tetto (f)
room	camera (f) or vano (m) or locale (m)
septic tank	fossa biologica (f)
service charges included	tariffe pubbliche comprese
study	studio (m)
supply (water, electricity)	alimentazione (f)
storeroom	ripostiglio (m)
swimming pool	piscina (f)

Lexicon: gli esperti – the experts

estimate	preventivo (m)
land ownership map	mappa (f) catastale
planning brief	PRG (piano regolatore generale)
surveyor	geometra (m)
valuer	consulente immobiliare

02

la vendita –
the sale

Almost the same...

When you buy a house in England or Wales, nothing is certain until you exchange contracts, close to the end of the process. In Italy you and the seller are both committed to the terms of the sale at the very beginning. You cannot be gazumped in Italy, neither buyer nor seller can renegotiate the price, nor can either of you back out without paying hefty compensation. A sale may be cancelled, but only if agreed conditions are not met or if a mortgage cannot be obtained. The whole process should take two to three months – about the same time as in the UK.

The role of an Italian lawyer, a *notaio*, is subtly different from that of a UK solicitor. A *notaio* is not there to represent your interests, but to ensure that the transfer of ownership is done fairly and properly – which is, of course, in your interests. It is quite normal for both parties to use the same *notaio* – there is no conflict involved, and there is less chance of communication problems and delays. If you want your own *notaio*, that is perfectly acceptable, and won't make any difference to the fees.

The *agente immobiliare* may play a different role here, too. They can take on the responsibility for checking the legal status of the property, e.g. that it is registered at the *catasto* (land registry) to the owner, and registered as residential, or if not, that permission can be obtained to convert it into a residence; that there are no outstanding mortgages on the property, or rights-of-way across it, or other rights owned by others over it. (These checks may done instead or as well by the *notaio*.) As the estate agents are so central to the property transfer, it is essential that they are competent and can be relied upon. Do ensure that your agent has the proper certification!

There are some differences on mortgages too. The authorities in Italy are more concerned than those in the UK that people should not over-extend themselves. Italian banks will lend you a smaller proportion of the value of the property, and take your main outgoings as well as your income into account when calculating the maximum loan.

La proprietà e la legge – ownership and the law

Who will own your house? And what do you want to happen when the owner or one of the owners dies? These are important questions because Italian property is subject to Italian inheritance law, even if you live in the UK.

Under Italian law, if you die without leaving a will, your property will be divided according to fixed ratios between your spouse and children, or your siblings and parents if there are no children. And your UK will does not count here – under English law, a UK will cannot deal with property overseas. Your Italian house must be disposed of through an Italian will. This need not be complicated, and there are no restrictions on who can inherit what – unlike French law, for example, where a spouse and any children must receive at least a minimum share. The other good news is that there are no inheritance taxes in Italy.

When you are buying you property, ask the *notaio* to draw up a will for you. A simple will costs little – especially compared to the cost and bother that will be incurred by your heirs if you don't have one.

Take expert advice

In all matters legal and financial, this book aims to give general guidance only. If you have any doubts or queries about what is right for you, talk to a properly qualified Italian specialist before making any decisions.

L'offerta d'acquisto – the offer to buy

Having found a house that you like and agreed a price with the vendor, it's time to start the buying process. At the first stage, the *agente immobiliare* may ask you for a deposit of between €1,000 to €10,000, as a sign of your commitment to the deal. The agent will then start work preparing the paperwork and the property should be taken off the market. Note however, that this only commits you – the vendor could, in theory, still accept other offers. Check with the agent about the vendor's commitment. If you pull out after signing this, you will lose the deposit. If the vendor withdraws, or the sale is cancelled for any other reason, your deposit will be refunded. When the sale moves to the next stage, the money will become part of your deposit on the house.

Proposta irrevocabile d'acquisto – irrevocable agreement to buy

The initial deposit will not secure the house indefinitely. If you need time to organise the money for the *compromesso* deposit (see below), and want to ensure that the property is taken off the market and stays off, you can sign a *proposta irrevocabile d'acquisto* (irrevocable agreement to buy) with your vendor. The vendor will probably want a larger deposit to agree to this, but it will be rolled over into the *compromesso* deposit later.

Il contratto preliminare – the pre-sale agreement

Also called *compromesso* (agreement), this is the most commonly used form of initial contract. There are alternatives including *contratto* or *accordo di compravendita* (sale contract or agreement). They share the same principles and have similar characteristics.

The contract must contain the following information:

- A description of the property, its dimensions and that of any related land. It may be necessary to hire a *geometra* (surveyor) to establish boundaries and ownership.

- If the property is an apartment, the contract should clearly identify the *aree comuni* (communal areas) and the *aree private* (areas private to the the owner).

- The actual price to be paid – not the taxable price (see *Il contratto di compravendita* below). If it is a new property, bought off-plan, payments may be made in stages as the building progresses.

- The amount of the deposit

- A date for signing the deed of sale.

The contract may also contain *clausole condizionali* (conditions – see page 37), and should list any rights of way or similar rights held by others over the land.

The initial contract is legally binding on both parties, and will have a *clausola penale* (penalty clause). If you pull out of the purchase, the deposit will be paid to the vendor as compensation. If the sellers withdraw from the sale, they must pay you an amount equal to the deposit, and your deposit is returned.

It isn't necessary for a *notaio* to be involved in drawing up the *contratto* – but it is better if one is, the *notaio* takes on the responsiblity of checking the property registration, and ensuring that it is free of mortgages, rights of way, etc. If anything does go wrong later, it will be much easier to get compensation.

The deposit, which can be anything from 15% to 50% of the price, is due on signature. It must be in euros, and if you do not yet have a Italian bank account, immediate payment may prove impossible. This should not be a problem. You can agree to pay within a set time, paying by bank transfer once you get back to the UK.

If you are using a *mutuo* (loan) or *ipoteca* (mortgage) to finance the purchase, the known details – how much you are borrowing and where you hope to borrow from – will be written into the contract. If you are, in the end, unable to obtain a mortgage, this will usually be accepted as a valid reason for not completing a sale – but ensure that this is specified in the contract.

You will be asked to make a *dichiarazione di domicilio* (statement of residence). This is for tax purposes – if this will be your primary residence, you will be subject to Italian income tax and social security contributions. If it is a secondary residence, you will only be liable for taxes on the property (see page 42).

Can your Italian cope?

You need good Italian to be able to cope with the legal and technical terminology in the contract. If you have any doubts about your ability to fully understand the documents, ask for copies, take them away and get them translated. Take advice from an English-speaking *notaio* or a UK solicitor who understands Italian law. Don't sign anything lightly.

Clausole condizionali – conditions

If you are going to take out a mortgage, then the contract is automatically dependent upon achieving that, but you can also write into the contract other conditions which must be met for the contract to be valid. These might include the receipt of a satisfactory *permesso di costruzione* (building permit) for your proposed building or rebuilding – this can take a while to come through (see Chapter 3), but if you want to do major work to the property you must be sure that you will be allowed to do it before you complete the sale. Any conditions must be agreed by the vendor, and time limits will be imposed, if appropriate. Be realistic. It can take time to get full, detailed planning permission through (see Chapter 3).

Registration

If there may be a significant delay before the completion of the sale, you can safeguard your purchase by registering the compromesso at the local Registration Tax Office. There is a small charge for this, but it will prevent a fraudulent vendor from selling the property again.

Your Italian finances

At some point in the two or three months between signing the *contratto preliminare* and the *contratto di compravendita* (contract of sale), you will need to organise your Italian finances. There are three key aspects to this.

Codice fiscale – tax ID

You must have an Italian tax code to be able to buy property in Italy. Contact the tax office while you are in Italy, or the Italian Consulate when you return home.

Bank account

You must have an Italian bank account to buy property in Italy, but even if it was not required, you would want one anyway. It makes life so much simpler. With a Italian account you can set up direct debits to pay the tax and utility bills and save a lot of trouble – being out of the country at the time is not an acceptable excuse for not paying a bill when it is due! It takes minutes to open an account. All you need is your passport and your intended address in Italy – you don't even need to put in any money. They will arrange to send correspondence to your UK address for as long as required.

Transferring money from the UK

When you are back home you can move cash from your UK bank, converted into euros, into your Italian account using Swift interbank transfer. Take the account details into the branch with you when you do this – they need your account's IBAN (International Bank Account Number). Make sure that you do this well before the time that the money is needed in Italy. In theory, the transfer will take between three and five days, but in practice it can be seven days or more – as long as everything goes smoothly, and errors are quite common. If you are in a rush, there is a 'same-day' transfer which should ensure that the money gets there within two to three days. Start the transfer process well in advance of the date of completion, and check that it has arrived in your Italian account before you leave the country.

* Unless you have enough cash to cover the purchase, its associated fees and charges, and the costs of settling into your new home, you will also need to arrange a mortgage in Italy or in the UK. We will return to these aspects of finance shortly.

Il contratto di compravendita – the contract of sale

Also referred to as *il rogito* or *atto notarile* (notarial deed), this is the document that transfers ownership, and has to be made in front of a *notaio*. The contract will later be registered in the *Conservatoria dei Registri Immobiliari* (Property Registration Office) and the price given here is the one on which government taxes and fees are calculated. It is normal for *valore catastale* (official value, set by the local registration office) to be different from the purchase price, though the differences are less than they used to be as the government is clamping down on this form of tax-dodging.

The *atto* is signed, with something of a ceremony, in the *notaio*'s office. Both the vendor and the purchaser are supposed to be there, though others can be given the power of attorney to sign for them. The *notaio* will read through the document. Then the balance of the purchase price will be handed over to the vendor. Next, the vendor and purchaser both initial each page and sign the last page, to show that they have understood the document and that they agree its terms. It is then countersigned by the *notaio* and stamped. Unless your Italian is very good, you are not likely to follow the reading very well, but you should have understand the document from working on it at the draft stage. If required, the *notaio* can arrange for a translator to be present.

La procura – the power of attorney

If it is not convenient for you to go – perhaps at very short notice – to the *notaio*'s office to sign the contract, you can give someone a power of attorney to sign for you. This is quite commonly done by the Italian themselves. The power of attorney is typically assigned to one of the clerks, though never to the *notaio*. The document to set up the power of attorney must comply with Italian requirements, but is then signed before a notary public in the UK, to be authenticated.

That is the end of the ceremony, but the transfer is not quite complete yet. The *notaio* will send the signed deed to the Property Registration Office, and around three weeks later you should get the title deed document.

Lexicon: i contratti – the contracts

accordo (m) d'acquisto	agreement to buy
accordo di compravendita	sale agreement
accordo di vendita	sale agreement
acquirente (m)	purchaser
acquisto (m)	purchase
aree comuni (m)	communal areas
aree private	private areas (in apartment block)
atto di cessione (m)	deed transfering property
atto notarile (m)	deed drawn up by a notaio
atto privato (m)	private agreement, alternative initial contract

catasto (m)	local register of land holdings
certificato d'acquisto	certificate of purchase
certificato urbanistico	town planning zoning certificate
clausola penale (f)	penalty clause
clausole condizionali	conditions to be met for the agreement to be valid
codice fiscale	tax ID
compromesso (m)	contract
compromesso preliminare	draft contract
comproprietà (f)	joint ownership
Conservatoria dei Registri Immobiliari	Property Registration Office
contratto (m)	contract
contratto di compravendita	contract of sale
contratto preliminare	pre-sale agreement
descrizione (f) dell' immobile	description of the property
dichiarazione (f) di domicilio	statement of residence
geometra (m)	surveyor
iscrizione di proprietà (f)	registration of ownership
mappa (f) catastale	map showing land ownership
notaio (m)	notary, lawyer and public official
offerta (f) d'acquisto	offer to buy (at a stated price)
proposta irrevocabile d'acquisto	irrevocable agreement to buy
rogito (m)	deed of sale
venditore (m)	seller
vendita (f)	sale

Beware the neighbours!

Take care when buying rural properties. If your neighbours are registered farmers they have the right to buy the property from you within one year of the purchase, and at the price declared in the deeds – which may be below the actual price, and will certainly be less than the total costs.

Aspetti finanziari – finance

L' ipoteca – the mortgage

Italian mortgages usually require foreign residents to provide at least 30%, and possibly 50%, of the purchase price. If the Italian property will be your main home, then a mortgage of up to 90% is possible. It can take up to two months to complete the loan – longer in the summer when many people are on holiday. The money will be released in two tranches: the first (typically no more than €75,000) on signing the deed of sale, and the rest after the deed has been recorded at the registration office.

There are some additional costs to factor into your budget.

- You must have life insurance to cover the mortgage – this will typically cost around 0.5% of the amount;

- the bank will charge approximately 0.5% for arranging the mortgage;

- the bank will insist on a survey, and you will be responsible for the surveyor's fee.

- there will be a tax of 2%, due on signing the deed of sale.

The mortgage offer will be no more than 60% or 70% of the surveyor's estimate of the value, which may well be less than the purchase price. For example, you may be asking for a mortgage for a property that you are buying for €100,00. The surveyor's estimate may value it at €80,000 and the bank may offer you as little as 50% of this – €40,000. At best, with a generous estimate and offer, you are unlikely to get a mortgage much over €60,000 for a second home in Italy.

Do you have the cash?

The mortgage can only cover the property itself, not the legal costs of buying it (up to 20%, see page 43), so you must have the cash for these too. For example, with a €100,000 house you would need at least €15,000 for the deposit and €18,000 for the fees and taxes. With all the other inevitable costs of moving and settling, you would be ill-advised to start out on the venture without at least €40,000 to hand.

If you take out an Italian mortgage, do bear in mind that not only do interest rates vary, exchange rates also vary. Interest rates are currently lower than in the UK. Four years ago the interest rate in Italy was around 4% and the exchange rate was £1 = €1.60. At the time of writing the interest rate is around 3% and the exchange rate is £1 = €1.45. According to the papers, the pound is overvalued, and the interest rate could go either way. A 25-year €100,000 mortgage now costs around £4,000 p.a. An increase of 1% in the interest rate, would increase it by a little over £400. A fall to 1.3 in the exchange rate would cost almost exactly the same.

If you have plenty of equity in your UK house, you could remortgage it to release funds for an outright purchase in Italy. If you do this, you must organise the remortgage before signing the initial contract, or have a clause written into it to cover the possibility of the remortgage not going through.

Whatever you do, take good advice and compare costs.

Fees and charges

Notaios perform a public function, and their fees are set by the state. They are non-negotiable, and there's no point in trying to shop around for a cheaper alternative. As transfer tax, registration costs and other official charges are also paid via the *notaio*, the total bill can be significant.

The fees and charges depend largely upon three things: the age of the property, its price and whether or not there is a mortgage.

* New properties are subject to *IVA* (VAT) currently at 9%, or 19% for luxury homes.

* *Imposti sulla cessione di immobili* (transfer taxes): *imposta di registro* (land registration tax) depends upon where the property is, and who you are. For urban properties, the tax is usually 4% for residents, or 10% for a non-resident buyer; in rural areas the tax will be up to 17%. *Imposta catastale* (registration tax) is an additional 1%. And note that the amounts are calculated on the declared value.

* The *notaio*'s fee is calculated from the price of the house – roughly 2.5% of the declared value, with a minimum of €1,000.

- The *agente immobiliare*'s fee is also calculated from the price of the house – typically 4% of the purchase price, or 3% on properties over €100,000. The seller usually pays half of this.

- If there is a mortgage, it is subject to *imposta ipotecaria* (mortgage tax) of 2%.

- If a *geometra* (surveyor) has been employed, the fee will be between €500 and €1000.

- You may also have needed the services of a translator and an accountant (it can be handy to have someone who really understands the local financial system). Allow €250 for each of these.

- VAT (currently 19%) is due on the *notaio*'s and *agente*'s fees.

For example, a rural property of €100,000 with declared value of €60,000 and a €50,000 mortage could result in these fees and charges:

Parcella notaio (notary fees)	€1,500
Commissione d'agenzia (agent's fees)	€3,000
IVA (VAT)	€855
Imposta di registro (land registration tax)	€10,200
Imposta catastale (registration tax)	€600
Imposta ipotecaria (mortgage tax)	€1,000
Geometra (surveyor)	€750
Other fees	€500
TOTALE ONERI (total fees)	€18,405

If you were buying an urban property of the same value, with the intention of becoming a resident, the land registration tax would have only been €2,400, bringing the total cost down to just over €10,000.

Italian taxes

There are three annual taxes, not all of which may apply. It is your responsibility to contact an accountant to determine the yearly tax bill.

Imposta comunale immobili – local property tax

The ICI (known as the 'Ichy') is an annual property tax, of approximately 0.6% of the declared price of the property, and is paid in two instalments, due in June and December.

Rifiuti solidi urbani – local refuse collection tax

Another local tax, typically around half the ICI.

IRPEF – income tax

If you own a house in Italy you must submit annual income tax accounts – though no tax will be due if there is no rental income from the house.

Lexicon: finance – aspetti finanziari

assicurazione (f)	insurance
commissione d'agenzia (f)	agency fees
imposta (f)	tax
imposta comunale immobili	local property tax
imposta di registro	land registration tax
imposta ipotecaria	mortgage tax
ipotecaria (f)	mortgage
mutuo (m)	mortgage
ordine (m) di addebito diretto	direct debit order
parcella notaio (m)	notary's fees
rifiuti solidi urbani	local refuse collection tax

I servizi – services

Apart from water, utilities in Italy are all supplied by state-owned companies. The services are good, and the costs are comparable to or cheaper than in the UK.

The utilities that are already connected to your house should be transferred to your name by the *agente immobiliare* or *notaio* handling the sale. If they don't provide this service for you, contact the vendor and get the details of their contracts. It should be simple enough to have the contracts transferred to your name at the appropriate time. Getting connected to mains water, electricity, gas or telephone for the first time may be a bit more involved and take a little longer to achieve.

Electricity is supplied by *ENEL (Ente Nazionale per l'Energia Elettrica S.p.A)*. Currently the annual standing charge is €75, and the cost per unit depends upon the level of consumption, falling from €0.20 to €0.10 per kW as more is used.

The electrical supply is 230 volts, as it is in the UK, but you will need to buy adaptors – or change the plugs – to be able to use UK appliances in round-pin sockets. Buy Italian, it's easier!

You can find out more about ENEL online at **http://www.enel.it**. You will need good Italian to make sense of this though – the 'English' link on the home page leads to a limited set of pages, mainly intended for overseas investors, not customers.

Mains gas is also supplied by ENEL, but at rates that vary by area – currently between €0.50 and €1.50 per kW. Note that many rural properties are not on the mains gas supply.

If you decide that you need a landline **telephone** you should talk to *Telecom Italia*. There will be an activation fee of €150, then a monthly standing charge of €15, plus usage costs. ISDN lines are available if needed, at comparable prices to those in the UK. Telecom Italia can be found online at **http://www.telecomitalia.it**. Again, you will need good Italian here – as with ENEL, the English parts of the site are for investors, not potential customers.

Your *acqua* (**water**) will be supplied by one of several companies – though there is no choice here, as only one is available in any area. The supply is metered, and the costs vary slightly. If your house is *collegata alla rete fognaria* (on mains drains), there will be an additional charge for waste water.

In towns, *l'immondizia* (**refuse**) is collected from your *bidone* (rubbish bin) inside your apartment block several times a week – daily in big cities. In the countryside it is collected from in front of your house.

Riciclaggio (recycling) provision varies, as it does in the UK. In many large cities there is now *raccolta differenziata* ('kerbside' or 'separate' recycling). In the countryside, as well as in munipical and supermarket car parks, you will find *campane per la raccolta del vetro* (bottle banks) and collection bins for paper, cardboard, cans, plastic bottles, textiles, batteries, and garden waste.

Old furniture, appliances, building detritus, hazardous materials and the like can all be disposed of in your local *deposito dei rifiuti* (waste disposal site) or *discarica* (dump).

Ask at the *comune* to find out your collection days or to locate your nearest recycling points.

Lexicon: i servizi – services

acqua (f)	water
bidone dell'immondizia (f)	rubbish bin
campana (f) per la raccolta del vetro	bottle bank
collegata alla rete fognaria pubblica	on mains drains
comune (m)	local council
deposito dei rifiuti (f)	waste collection site
discarica (f)	rubbish dump
elettricità (f)	electricity
municipio (m)	town hall (the building itself)
Pagine Gialle	Yellow Pages
raccolta differenziata	'separate' recycling
riciclaggio (m)	recycling
rifiuti (m)	rubbish

English–Italian quick reference

The contracts – i contratti

agreement	accordo (m)
agreement to buy	accordo d'acquisto
certificate of purchase	certificato d'acquisto
aree (m) comuni	communal areas

conditional clause	clausole (m) condizionali
contract	compromesso (m), contratto (m)
contract of sale	contratto di compravendita
deed of sale	atto (m) notarile/di cessione
description of the property	descrizione (f) dell'immobile
draft contract	compromesso preliminare
joint ownership	comproprietà (f)
land ownership map	mappa (f) catastale
notary	notaio (m)
offer to buy	offerta (f) d'acquisto
penalty clause	clausola (f) penale
pre-sale agreement	contratto preliminare
private agreement	atto privato (m)
private areas in block	aree (m) private
purchase	acquisto (m)
purchaser	acquirente (m)
register of land holdings	catasto (m)
registration of ownership	iscrizione di proprietà (f)
sale	vendita (f)
sale agreement	accordo (m) di vendita/ compravendita
seller	venditore (m)
statement of residence	dichiarazione (f) di domicilio
surveyor	geometra (m)
town planning certificate	certificato urbanistico

Lexicon: finance – aspetti finanziari

agency fees	commissione d'agenzia (f)
direct debit order	ordine (m) di addebito diretto
insurance	assicurazione (f)
land registration tax	imposta di registro
local property tax	imposta comunale immobili
mortgage	ipotecaria (f), mutuo (m)

mortgage tax   imposta ipotecaria
notary's fees   parcella notaio (m)
refuse collection tax   rifiuti solidi urbani
tax   imposta (f)

Services – i servizi

bottle banks   campane per la raccolta del vetro
electricity   elettricità (f)
on mains drains   collegata alla rete fognaria
                            pubblica
recycling   riciclaggio (m)
rubbish   rifiuti (m)
rubbish bin   bidone dell'immondizia (m)
rubbish dump   discarica (f)
town hall   comune (m)
waste collection site   deposito dei rifiuti (m)
water   acqua (f)
Yellow Pages   Pagine Gialle

03

i lavori –
building work

Almost the same...

The Italians have planning permission and building regulations the same as we do in the UK, only more so. You must have permission to build, convert or extend a property, and if it is in near a historic building or anywhere in a protected town or a area of the countryside, you may be very restricted in what you can build, where, its size, style, materials and even colour.

In other books in this series, we have gone into some detail on the forms that you need to fill in and processes that you must follow to get planning permission. We are not going to go into the same details here. This is not because there aren't forms and processes – on the contrary, Italian bureaucracy is legendary and they have a myriad of laws that can affect any given application. It's not worth spending your time and our space on the details because getting planning permission is just not something that amateurs – especially foreigner amateurs – should attempt. You need a local professional – an *architetto* (architect) or *geometra* (surveyor) – to do it for you. Only they know the right way through the bureaucracy and the right people to talk to. What follows is a just brief guide to put you in the picture.

Check at the comune

The *comune* is central to all this. It's where the planning permits are issued, and it's where you should be able to find lists of tradesmen. In smaller communities, the *sindaco* (mayor) in person may play a significant role in this. It can take a longer or shorter time to get permissions agreed, and there can be more or fewer nits picked in the process. If you work with the *comune* and the officials, and show that you want to be part of their community, it should help things go more smoothly. Even so, it can take some months – even years – to get planning permission, especially if the property is in any kind of historic area.

Depending upon the size of your *comune*, there may be an *architetto consulente* (consultant architect) or other qualified officer who can advise you on the regulations and how they apply to your project.

Il piano regolatore generale – the planning brief

Almost all *comuni* have a PRG (*piano regolatore generale*) or planning brief – a map and a planning brief that determines what use can be made of the land. If you are buying a building plot, or a ruin that you intend to rebuild, check the P.R.G. map to make sure that such development is possible in that area. If you are buying in town, it's as well to check that any future developments won't alter the character of the neighbourhood.

Ask at the *comune* to see the PRG. The town's surveyor should be happy to show it to you.

Planning controls

What form of permit is needed depends mainly upon the nature of the project. Your building professional will advise you on what is required, but these guidelines generally apply:

* If you are going to build a new house, extend an existing one outwards or upwards, add a garage, a substantial outbuilding or a swimming pool, you will need either a *permesso di costruzione* (building permit) or a *concessione edilizia* (planning permission) – or possibly both.

* If the work is purely internal, or has only minimal impact on the outside of the house, e.g. a new window, then a *denuncia di inizio attività* (notice of works) may be sufficient.

* If you are installing a new bathroom or toilet, or making other changes to the sanitation, these must meet the *USL (Unità Sanitaria Locale)* regulations.

* Minor internal work does not require any permissions, but must still meet building regulations on things like minimal ceiling height (2.7 m, in case you are interested).

Permissions are all handled through the *comune*. If the work is subject to a *denuncia di inizio attività* (notice of works), the application *modulo* (form) should be submitted, with the plans, a month before the work is to start. If the *comune* has raised no objections by the end of the month, you can go ahead.

Getting a *permesso di costruzione* (building permit) is more complex and more expensive. You will need properly drawn-up plans for a start, which is another reason for hiring a professional, and will have to pay a tax of 5% of the building costs. The application will be passed on to the *Commissione Edilizia* (Building Commission) for checking and approval. If the house is in a historic area, additional checking and permissions will be necessary. It will be a minimum of two months before approval is given – even if everything goes well and no changes to the plans are requested. It can take years.

Welcome, benvenuto

If a council wants to encourage people to buy and restore properties in the area, it may simplify and speed up the planning approval process. Some also waive the tax.

Assuming that you get approval, when the work is completed, you should register the new house plans with the *Conservatorio dei Registri Immobiliari* (Property Registration Office). Failure to do so could create problems if and when you try to sell the house.

I professionisti – the professionals

L'architetto – architect

If you intend to build a house from scratch, or do a substanital extension on an existing house, you will need to employ an *architetto* (architect). As well as drawing up plans, and handling the planning permission application, they can also organise and oversee the tradesmen when you get the go-ahead. An *architetto* will typically charge around 7.5% of the cost of the job to draw up plans, and another 7.5% to organise the construction.

Il geometra – the surveyor

For renovation work or small extensions, a *geometra* may be better – and his fees will almost certainly be cheaper – than an *architetto*. They can draw up plans of existing buildings and of their modifications, and will normally have good local contacts among the tradesmen and with the *comune*. A good *geometra* should be able to draw on a wide knowledge of materials and techniques to suggest solutions that you wouldn't have thought of yourself.

If you want to have the work done while you are in the UK, then employing a *geometra* is a sensible solution even for the simpler jobs. Even if you are there yourself, employing a *geometra* should ensure that the job is done better, and the extra cost may not be that much in the long run.

Gli operai – the tradesmen

For work that does not need planning permission, decorating, internal woodwork, refurbished kitchen, or similar jobs, and where you have the time and confidence to oversee the job yourself, you may prefer to hire trademen directly. How can you find the good ones?

Start by asking at the *agenzia immobiliare*. They should be able to recommend tradesmen, and may be able to put you in touch with other recent clients who have had similar work done. The *comune* may also be able to give you a list of local tradesmen.

The informal quality checks work as well, or better, in Italy as in the UK especially in the rural areas. Tradesmen prefer to work in their local area, and to rely more on word of mouth than advertising for their business, so reputation is important. Ask your neighbours if they can recommend people for the work.

Keep an eye out for the names of builders on the notices where building is in progress. And if all else fails, Italy has *Pagine Gialle* (Yellow Pages) just as we do. The numbers given here are often home numbers, which means that they are most likely to be there at lunchtime and after 7.0 or 8.00 in the evening.

DIY at your own risk!

By Italian law, all building work has to be guaranteed for 2 years provided the fault is reported within 60 days. As part of this, the trademen have to carry their own insurance to cover their work. If you have the work done 'on the black' – cash in hand – you will not have those guarantees.

Il preventivo – the estimate

A *preventivo* (estimate) should be taken as exactly that – an estimated price, not the actual one. The quote may be given in the form of a *forfait* (price for the whole job), or a *misura* (price per square metre). For some restoration work, the trademen may only be willing to give you a price *in economia* (an hourly rate). On any building project it is always wise to assume that unforeseen hitches will push the price up by 20% or so.

But do be clear about what you are asking for. There have been cases of people getting a *preventivo* for a bathroom to find that it only included equipment and delivery. If you want it *tutto in opera* (fitting) and *funzionante* (working), make sure that this is specified in the *preventivo*!

L'abbattimento dell' IVA – reduced VAT

Building work is taxed at a reduced rate of 4%, instead of the normal 19%. If you are doing the work yourself, you may be able to claim this rate for any materials that you buy. Ask at the *comune* about getting the necessary certification.

Other trades

- *capomastro* – 'master of the works', the person in charge of a building site

- *costruttore edile* – builder, general term

- *muratore* – bricklayer

- *intonacatore* – plasterer

- *falegname* – carpenter, specialising in roof timbers

- *copritetto* – roofer, working with tiles, slates or similar

- *carpentiere* – joiner, for windows, doors, etc

- *idraulico* – plumber

- *elettricista* – electrician

We will meet these and other tradesmen in the rest of the book.

Lexicon: i lavori – building work

abbattimento dell' IVA	reduced rate of VAT on building work and materials
architetto consulente	consultant architect
cantiere (m)	building site
capomastro	master of the works, project manager for building work
Commissione Edilizia	Building Commission responsible for planning applications
concessione edilizia	planning permission
Conservatoria dei Registri Immobiliari	Property Registration Office
costruttore edile (m)	builder, general term
denuncia d'inizio attività	notice of starting work
geometra (m)	surveyor
modulo (m)	form
operaio (m)	tradesman
permesso di costruzione	permit...
piano regolatore generale	local planning brief for land use
preventivo (m)	estimate
... a forfait	... for complete job
... a misura	... as price per square metre
... in economia	... as an hourly rate
sindaco (m)	mayor
Unità Sanitaria Locale	sanitary regulations

English–Italian quick reference

architect	architetto (m)
builder	costruttore edile (m)
building site	cantiere (m)
consultant architect	architetto consulente
estimate	preventivo (m)
... an hourly rate	... in economia

... price per square metre	... a misura
... complete job	... a forfait
form	modulo (m)
land use brief	piano regolatore generale (PRG)
mayor	sindaco (m)
project manager	capomastro (m)
notice of starting work	denuncia d'inizio attività
building permit	permesso di costruzione
planning permission	concessione edilizia
sanitary regulations	Unità Sanitaria Locale (USL)
surveyor	geometra (m)
tradesman	operai (m)

04

la struttura –
the structure

Almost the same...

The Italians seem to be very keen on preserving regional identities in their housing. This is less so in the larger towns and cities, but in smaller places – especially in the more picturesque areas – the houses typically all have the same look. You will find white-washed houses throughout the South and Sardinia, and red tiled roofs over pastel-coloured walls in central and northern Italy. In the far north, on the border with Switzerland, broad roofs overhang the balconies around wooden chalets. And in the southern region of Apulia, at Alberobello, you will find some of the most unusual constructions in Europe: *trulli* – ancient white-washed buildings made of stone, formed by a circular base and a cone-shaped *cupola*.

And the regional look is often not just a matter of preference. We have listed buildings and preservation areas in the UK, and so do the Italians. But they go further. The Italians believe that, though the house may belong to you, its external appearance is a matter of common concern. If you plan to build a new house, or make changes to an existing one, and want yours to stand out from its neighbours, think again. You can have your individuality, but it must be within the limits of the regional look.

On a purely practical level, all old Italian houses – and many new ones – have solid walls. Cavity walls are not standard, as they are in the UK. The walls of new houses are often built of hollow red bricks, which are large and light and go up very quickly. With rendering on the outside and insulated plasterboard on the inside, these have reasonable insulating qualities.

Check at the comune

- If you are planning any change to the outside of the house, talk to the planning officer at the *comune* at an early stage – see Chapter 3.

- The *comune* should have a list of registered tradesmen in your area.

La struttura – the structure

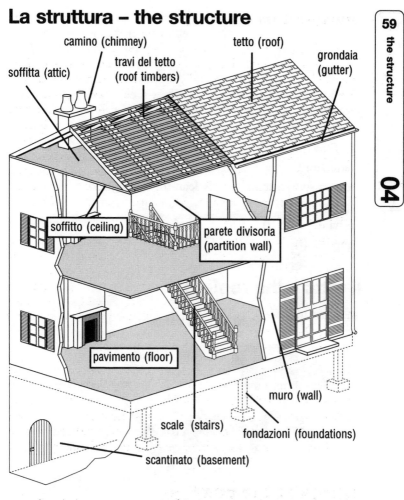

camino (chimney)

tetto (roof)

grondaia (gutter)

soffitta (attic)

travi del tetto (roof timbers)

soffitto (ceiling)

parete divisoria (partition wall)

pavimento (floor)

muro (wall)

scale (stairs)

fondazioni (foundations)

scantinato (basement)

camino (m)	chimney
fondazioni (f)	foundations – often absent from older houses
muffa (f)	mould
muro (m)	wall
parete divisoria (f)	partition wall
pavimento (m)	floor
pietrisco (m)	rubble

pozzo di luce (m)	light shaft – skylight over a stairwell or inner room
putrescenza (f)	rot
rifiuti (m)	rubbish
scale (m)	stairs
scantinato (m)	basement
soffitta (m)	attic/loft
soffitto (m)	ceiling
tetto (m)	roof
tetto a spiovente (m)	lean-to, sloping roof
tramezzo (m)	party wall
travi del tetto (f)	roof timbers
umidità (f)	mildew

Il tetto – the roofing

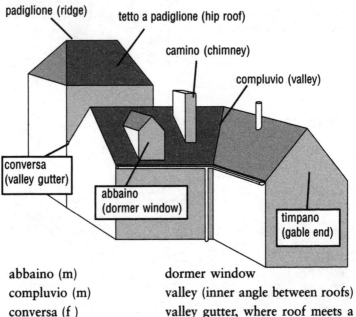

padiglione (ridge) tetto a padiglione (hip roof)

camino (chimney)

compluvio (valley)

conversa (valley gutter)

abbaino (dormer window)

timpano (gable end)

abbaino (m)	dormer window
compluvio (m)	valley (inner angle between roofs)
conversa (f)	valley gutter, where roof meets a second roof or a higher wall
fascia (f)	eaves board or fascia

feltro isolante (m)	lining felt
frontone (m)	pediment (wall higher than the end of the roof)
gronda	eaves
lucernaio (m)	(Velux) skylight
padiglione (f)	ridge
piccolo abbaino (m)	small dormer window
scossalina (f)	flashing
tetto a terrazza (m)	terrace roof
tetto a padiglione (m)	hip roof
timpano (m)	gable end

lucernaio (skylight)

Le travi del tetto – the roof timbers

In older houses and house with gables, the roof will normally be made from rafters on a ridge beam and wall plates, braced by horizontal beams. In other cases, ready-made triangular trusses will be used to create the basic structure.

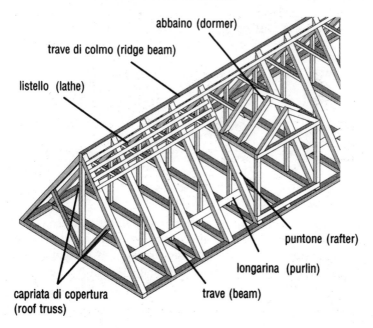

abbaino (dormer)

trave di colmo (ridge beam)

listello (lathe)

puntone (rafter)

longarina (purlin)

capriata di copertura (roof truss)

trave (beam)

abbaino (m)	dormer
arco del tetto (m)	roof arch
assicella (f)	batten
capriata di copertura (f)	roof truss
capriate prefabbricate (f)	small trusses, factory-made
castagna (f)	chestnut
conservante per legno (m)	wood preservative
listello (m)	lathe
longarina (f)	purlin (horizontal tie on rafters)
pino (m)	pine
puntone (m)	rafter
puntone di falda (m)	rafter as part of truss
quercia (f)	oak
trave orizzontale (f)	horizontal beam
trave di colmo	ridge beam
trave (f)	beam

An attic with *arco del tetto* (arches), like this one, will be easier to convert into a habitable room, than one where the roof is formed from trusses

Lathes and tiles

If the roof is to be covered with slates of flat tiles, these will be hung on lathes. Lathes are also used now with curved tiles, but on older houses you may find flat planking or triangular supports). The tiles are sometimes simply placed on top of these – not attached – and have a tendency to slip steadily down the roof over the years.

As in the UK, you will not find lining felt under the tiles of older houses, unless they have been reroofed recently.

Materiali di copertura del tetto – roofing materials

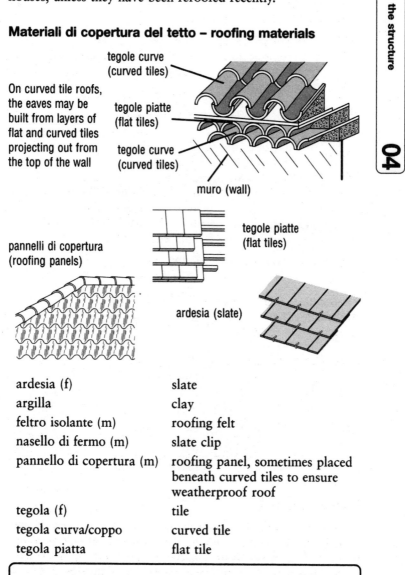

tegole curve
(curved tiles)

On curved tile roofs, the eaves may be built from layers of flat and curved tiles projecting out from the top of the wall

tegole piatte
(flat tiles)

tegole curve
(curved tiles)

muro (wall)

tegole piatte
(flat tiles)

pannelli di copertura
(roofing panels)

ardesia (slate)

ardesia (f)	slate
argilla	clay
feltro isolante (m)	roofing felt
nasello di fermo (m)	slate clip
pannello di copertura (m)	roofing panel, sometimes placed beneath curved tiles to ensure weatherproof roof
tegola (f)	tile
tegola curva/coppo	curved tile
tegola piatta	flat tile

If the *agenzia immobiliare*'s advert says '*tetto in buone condizioni*', all that means is that it doesn't leak – much.

64

la struttura

04

Roofing tradesmen

- If you want to build, adapt or mend the roofing timbers, you need a *falegname* (carpenter).

- To replace or mend a roof, you need a *copritetto* (roofer).

I muri – walls

Walls start from foundations, though not necessarily... In older houses, especially in country areas and where large stones were the building material, the walls were often built directly on the ground. Two possible problems can arise from this. You can get subsidence, though with an old house it's a reasonable bet that it has sunk as much as it's going to. You may also have rising damp, as there will be no barrier beneath the stones. The damp problem will be worse if the original – breathing – floor of beaten earth or flagstones has been replaced by concrete and tiles.

barriera impermeabile (f)	damp course
crepe (f)	cracks
edilizia (f)	building
fondazioni (f)	foundations
fossa (f)	trench
ricarica (f)	hardcore
riempire di calce le commessure	point – renew mortar of walls
muro (m)	wall
scavo (m)	excavation
umidità (f)	damp
umidità risalente (f)	rising damp

External walls

For new building, the Italian favour *mattoni* (hollow concrete or clay blocks). These come in a wide range of sizes and cross-sections, offering different weight to strength ratios. The resulting walls are not very attractive when bare, but they are not intended to remain bare as both the outside and the inside are normally rendered with mortar.

Where a wall is built with a cavity, the structure is usually different from in the UK. Here a cavity wall has an inner load-bearing skin of brick or breeze block, and an outer skin of brick. In Italy the cavity is formed by adding a thin inner skin to a standard thickness, load-bearing outer wall. Both inner and outer walls are often made of hollow bricks.

Some wall styles

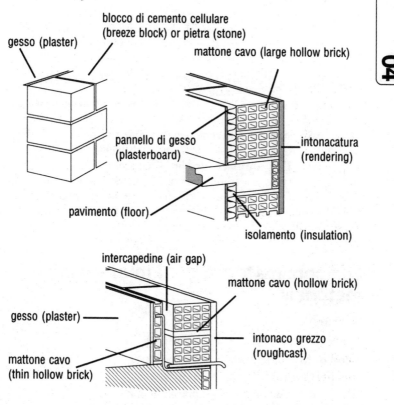

gesso (plaster)

blocco di cemento cellulare (breeze block) or pietra (stone)

mattone cavo (large hollow brick)

pannello di gesso (plasterboard)

intonacatura (rendering)

pavimento (floor)

isolamento (insulation)

intercapedine (air gap)

mattone cavo (hollow brick)

gesso (plaster)

intonaco grezzo (roughcast)

mattone cavo (thin hollow brick)

Instant walls!

If you want a very strong, solid wall quickly, build a dry wall – no mortar – of the hollowest bricks, slide reinforcing rods down through them, then fill with wet concrete.

Le pareti divisorie – partition walls

Some or all of the internal walls of a house may be *pareti divisorie*. Smaller farms and terraced houses in towns are often built with the floor and ceiling joists supported solely by the outside walls. Keep this in mind when you look around old houses. *Pareti divisorie* are easily removed and rebuilt elsewhere if you want to remodel the internal layout.

Old *pareti divisorie* are likely to be lathe and plaster or single-skin brick. New ones are quickly built from thin hollow bricks, plasterboard on wooden frames or plaster blocks.

Digression: blocchi di gesso – plaster blocks

You won't find these in the UK, but plaster blocks are worth investigating. They are typically 66 × 50 cm, in widths from 7 to 12 cm and come in different weights and finishes – including waterproof ones for bathrooms and lightweight ones for loft conversions. They are assembled like brickwork – but much easier and faster – need no framework and can be cut with a wood saw. Exposed corners can be reinforced with an angled metal strip, if required. After a little fine filling of the ends and joints, the new wall is ready for decorating.

Lexicon: materiali per i muri – wall materials

architrave (f)	lintel
arenaria (f)	sandstone
blocco (m) di cemento cellulare	breeze block
blocco di gesso (m)	plaster block
calcare (m)	limestone
calcestruzzo (m)	cement
cemento (m)	concrete
cemento armato (m)	reinforced concrete
cornice (f) perimetrale a L	angled (L-shaped) strip for reinforcing plaster corner
ferro di collegamento (m)	wall tie

granito (m)	granite
in legno e muratura (m)	half-timbered
intercapedine (f)	air gap – may contain insulation
intonacatura (f)	rendering
intonaco grezzo (m)	roughcast – external wall covering applied like plaster, or sprayed from a machine
isolamento (m)	insulation
malta (f)	mortar
mattone (m)	brick
mattone cavo	hollow brick
mattone refrattario	firebrick
pannello (m)	panel
pannello di gesso	plasterboard
pietra (f)	stone
pietra da taglio	quarry stone
pietra lavorata	dressed stone
rivestimento (m)	lining – could be plasterboard
sabbia (f)	sand
sabbia grezza	coarse sand

Isolamento – insulation

bordatura in gomma (f)	rubber beading
fibra di vetro	fibreglass
lana di roccia (f)	rockwool
pannello composito	composite panel – e.g. plasterboard backed with an insulating material
pannello isolante (m)	insulation panel
parafreddo (m)	draught-proofing
paraspifferi (m)	draught excluder
particelle di sughero (f)	cork particles
polistirolo (m)	polystyrene
poliuretano (m)	polyurethane
vermicolite (f)	mica particles

Building trademen

+ A builder is a *muratore* or a *costruttore*.
+ If you want a bricklayer, ask for a *muratore*.
+ If you want a stonemason, ask for a *scalpellino*.
+ For plastering, you need an *intonacatore*.

Gli attrezzi da muratore – builder's tools

Brickwork

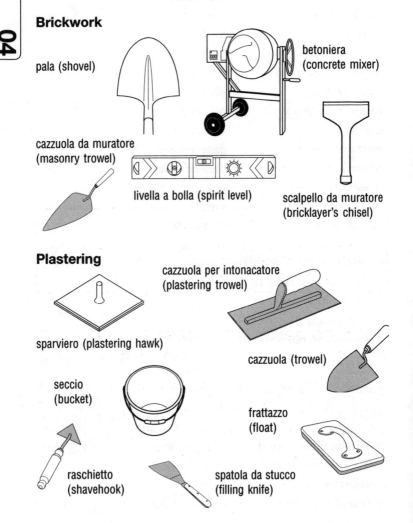

pala (shovel)

betoniera
(concrete mixer)

cazzuola da muratore
(masonry trowel)

livella a bolla (spirit level)

scalpello da muratore
(bricklayer's chisel)

Plastering

cazzuola per intonacatore
(plastering trowel)

sparviero (plastering hawk)

cazzuola (trowel)

seccio
(bucket)

frattazzo
(float)

raschietto
(shavehook)

spatola da stucco
(filling knife)

betoniera (m)	concrete mixer
cazzuola (f)	trowel
cazzuola da muratore	masonry trowel
cazzuola per intonacare	plastering trowel
crivello (m)	riddle – box with a mesh base for removing lumps and stones from sand or other dry material
frattazzo (m)	float
livella a bolla (f)	spirit level
pala (f)	shovel
piccone (m)	pick
raschietto (m)	shavehook (triangular scraper)
scalpello (m)	chisel
scalpello da muratore	bricklayer's chisel
secchio (f)	bucket
sparviero (m)	plastering hawk
spatola da stucco (f)	filling knife
vanga (f)	spade

Which word?

Sometimes there are several words for the same thing. Try to learn one well enough to be able to ask for it, and others well enough to recognise them when you hear them.

Soffitti e pavimenti – ceilings and floors

In older houses, the ceiling and floor are often – literally – two sides of the same thing! The traditional wooden floor consists of planks laid over joists, and the undersides of the planks form the ceiling. In houses without central heating, this allows the warmth from the downstairs living rooms to rise up to the bedrooms – but it also lets the noise up.

In apartments and in more modern houses, the floor will be made of reinforced concrete. Apart from better soundproofing, this

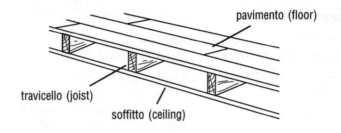

pavimento (floor)

travicello (joist)

soffitto (ceiling)

also allows the use of ceramic tiles for floors in upstairs rooms.
(You cannot lay hard tiles on flexible wood floors.)

listelli e gesso	lathe and plaster
pannellatura (m)	pannelling
pavimento (m)	floor
soffitto (m)	ceiling
travicello (m)	joist

English–Italian quick reference

The structure – la struttura

attic	soffitta (f)
basement	scantinato (m)l
ceiling	soffitto (m)
chimney	camino (m)
floor	pavimento (m)
foundations	fondazioni (f)
lean-to	tetto (m) a spiovente
mould	muffa (f)
party wall	tramezzo
rot	putrescenza (f)
rubbish	rifiuti (m)
rubble	pietrisco (m)
stairs	scale (f)
wall	muro (m)

The roof – il tetto

attic	soffitta (f)
beam	trave (f)
carpenter	falegname (m)
ceiling	soffitto (m)
chimney	camino (m)
clay	argilla (f)
dormer window	abbaino (m)
eaves	gronda (f)
flashing	scossalina (f)
gable	timpano (m)
hip roof	tetto (m) a padiglione
lathe	listello (m)
lining felt	feltro isolante (m)
oak	quercia (f)
pediment	frontone (m)
pine	pino (m)
rafter	puntone (m)
ridge	trave di colmo (f)
roof	tetto (m)
roof timbers	travi del tetto (m)
roof truss	capriata (f) di copertura
roofer	copritetto (m)
roofing felt	feltro isolante (m)
roofing panel	pannello di copertura (m)
skylight	lucernaio (m)
slate	ardesia (f)
slate clip	nasello di fermo (m)
sloping roof	tetto spiovente (m)
terrace roof	tetto a terrazza (f)
tile	tegola (f)
tile, curved	tegola curva/coppo
valley	compluvio (m)

valley gutter — conversa (f)

wood preservative — conservante per legno (m)

Walls – i muri

air gap — intercapedine (f)

breeze block — blocco di cemento cellulare (m)

brick — mattone (m)

brick, hollow — mattone cavo

bricklayer — muratore (m)

builder — costruttore (m)

building (work) — edilizia (f)

cement — calcestruzzo (m)

concrete — cemento (m)

concrete, reinforced — cemento armato

crack (in wall) — crepa (f)

damp — umidità (f)

damp course — barriera impermeabile (f)

excavation — scavo (m)

floor — pavimento (m)

foundations — fondazioni (f)

granite — granito (m)

half-timbered — costruzione in legno e muratura (f)

insulation — isolamento (m)

limestone — calcare (m)

lining (for wall) — rivestimento (m)

lintel — architrave (m)

mildew — umidità (f)

mortar — malta (f)

mould — muffa (f)

panel — pannello (m)

partition wall — tramezzo (m)

plaster — gesso (m)

plasterboard — pannello di gesso (m)

plaster block — blocco di gesso

plasterer	intonacatore (m)
point (walls)	riempire di calce le commessure
quarry stone	pietra da taglio (f)
rendering	intonacatura (m)
rising damp	umidità risalente (f)
rot	putrescenza (f)
roughcast	intonaco grezzo (m)
rubbish	rifiuti (m)
rubble	pietrisco (m)
sand	sabbia (m)
sandstone	arenaria (f)
stone	pietra (f)
stone, dressed	pietra lavorata
stonemason	scalpellino (m), tagliapetre (m)
trench	fossa (f)
wall	muro (m)
wall tie	ferro di collegamento (m)

Tools – gli attrezzi

bricklayer's chisel	scalpello da muratore (m)
bucket	secchio (m)
chisel	scalpello
concrete mixer	betoniera (f)
filling knife	spatola da stucco (f)
float	frattazzo (f)
pick	piccone (m)
plastering hawk	sparviero per intonacare (m)
plastering trowel	cazzuola per intonacare (f)
riddle	crivello (m)
shavehook	raschietto (m)
shovel	pala (f)
spade	vanga (f)
spirit level	livella a bolla (f)
trowel	cazzuola (f)

Ceilings and floors – soffitti e pavimenti

ceiling	soffitto (m)
floor	pavimento (m)
joist	travicello (m)
lathe and plaster	listelli e gesso
pannelling	pannellatura (f)

05

le opere in legno – woodwork

Almost the same...

In the UK, building professionals make a distinction between joinery or carpentry, though for most of us, it's all woodwork. The Italians make a similar distinction. If you want someone to make, fit or mend staircases, windows, doors and the like, you need *un falegname*.

The most obvious difference is in the windows. Most Italian houses have shutters. We're fans of shutters. They keep the sun out on a summer's day, the warmth in on a winter's night, and the burglars out at when you're away. A side effect of having shutters is that the windows must open inwards, or slide.

There's a small but significant difference in the way they hang doors – they use split hinges. We're fans of these too, and so will you be the next time that you are painting a door, laying floor tiles, moving big furniture or doing any other job where a door in a doorway is a nuisance. With split hinges, you just lift the door off and prop it up somewhere out of the way.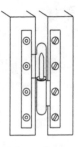

Split hinges make a simple job of hanging (and unhanging) doors – as long as you fit them the right way up!

Check at the comune

♦ Your internal fittings are entirely your affair, but if you are adding or altering external doors or windows – especially on the publicly-visible sides of the house – check with the *comune* if the new ones are different from the others in the neighbourhood.

Le opere in legno interne – internal woodwork

asse (m) del pavimento	floorboard
battiscopa (m)	skirting board
cimasa (f)	picture rail
controsoffitto (m)	false ceiling

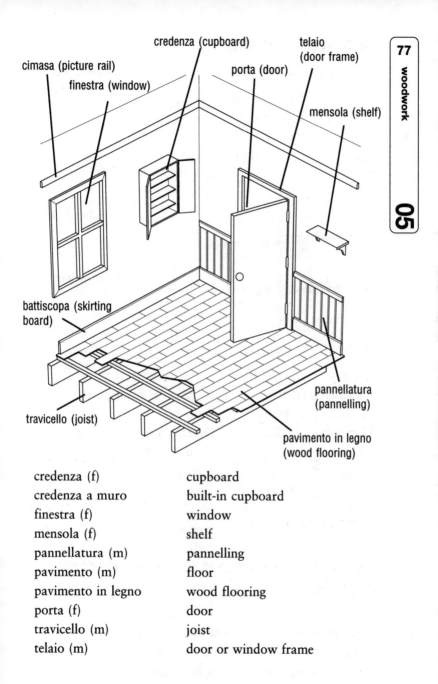

cimasa (picture rail)

finestra (window)

credenza (cupboard)

porta (door)

telaio (door frame)

mensola (shelf)

battiscopa (skirting board)

travicello (joist)

pannellatura (pannelling)

pavimento in legno (wood flooring)

credenza (f)	cupboard
credenza a muro	built-in cupboard
finestra (f)	window
mensola (f)	shelf
pannellatura (m)	pannelling
pavimento (m)	floor
pavimento in legno	wood flooring
porta (f)	door
travicello (m)	joist
telaio (m)	door or window frame

Le porte – doors

Italian doors are often sold ready-made in two forms:

* *Il blocco porta* (door block) consists of the door and its frame with the hinges and lock fitted.

* *La porta sola* (door alone) is just the door.

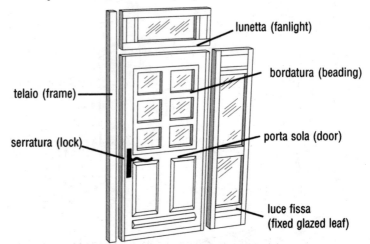

telaio (frame)

serratura (lock)

lunetta (fanlight)

bordatura (beading)

porta sola (door)

luce fissa
(fixed glazed leaf)

bordatura (f)	beading for fixing glass
cassetta delle lettere (f)	letter box
gruppo porta (m)	door with frame and fittings
luce fissa (f)	fixed glazed leaf
lunetta (f)	fanlight
pomello (da porta)	door knob
porta (f)	door
porta di sicurezza (f)	high-security (armoured) door
porta scorrevole (f)	sliding door
porta a vento (f)	swing door
soglia (f)	doorstep, sill
telaio (m)	frame

Serramenti per porte – hardware for doors

cerniera (f)	hinge
cerniera estraibile (f)	split hinge

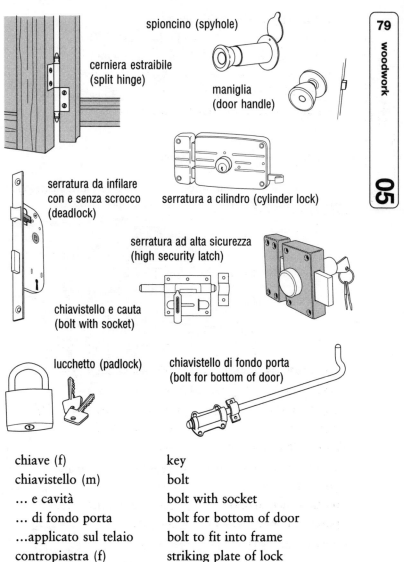

spioncino (spyhole)

cerniera estraibile
(split hinge)

maniglia
(door handle)

serratura da infilare
con e senza scrocco
(deadlock)

serratura a cilindro (cylinder lock)

serratura ad alta sicurezza
(high security latch)

chiavistello e cauta
(bolt with socket)

lucchetto (padlock)

chiavistello di fondo porta
(bolt for bottom of door)

chiave (f)	key
chiavistello (m)	bolt
… e cavità	bolt with socket
… di fondo porta	bolt for bottom of door
…applicato sul telaio	bolt to fit into frame
contropiastra (f)	striking plate of lock
fermo (m)	catch
foro (m) chiave	keyhole
lucchetto (m)	padlock
maniglia (f)	door handle

serratura (f)	lock
... a cilindro	cylinder lock
... ad alta sicurezza	high security latch
... da infilare	mortice lock
... da infilare con e senza scrocco	deadlock
spioncino (m)	spyhole for door

Le finestre – windows

Traditionally, windows are hinged and deep-set, and either open outwards – or, where there are shutters, open inwards.

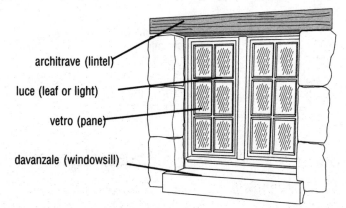

architrave (lintel)

luce (leaf or light)

vetro (pane)

davanzale (windowsill)

Other opening styles include:

+ *ad asse verticale apribile verso l'esterno* – hinged and opening outwards

+ *ad asse orizzontale inferiore* – hinged at the bottom, opening in and down

+ *basculante* – swivelling horizontally

+ *scorrevole* – sliding

basculante

scorrevole

La finestra – the window

architrave (f)	lintel
davanzale (m)	windowsill
doppi vetri	double glazing
finestra (f)	window
... a battente	casement window
... a bovindo	bay window
... a inferriata	lattice window
... a loggia sporgente	oriel window
... a lucernaio	skylight
luce (m)	leaf or light
porta-finestra (f)	french window
telaio (m)	window frame
vetro (m)	glass
vetro di finestra (m)	window pane
vetratura (f)	glazing
zanzariera (f)	mosquito net

Scuri e serrande avvolgibili – shutters

Shutters are fitted on doors and windows to give extra security, shade and insulation. There are many styles – in wood and other materials.

Scuri a battenti – hinged shutters

A *battenti* means that the shutters are hinged and open flat against the outside wall, where they are held by a *fermascuri* (catch). To secure the shutters when closed, they normally use a *spagnoletta* – a rod that holds the two leaves together and locks into the top and bottom of the frame.

Styles and shapes vary widely, depending on region or even town of use, i.e. *alla veneziana*, *padovana*, *vicentina*, *bolognese*, *ferrarese*, etc.

scuri in legno – solid wood shutter

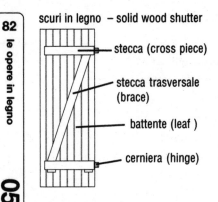

stecca (cross piece)

stecca trasversale (brace)

battente (leaf)

cerniera (hinge)

persiana – slatted shutter

Serrande avvolgibili – roller shutters

These are made from PVC or metal, not wood, but we're putting them here anyway! Roller shutters can be fitted inside the door or window frame, or project out from it. They can be hand-wound or electrically operated.

cassonetto coprirullo (casing)

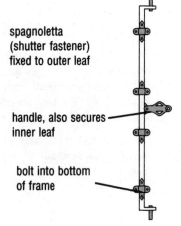

guide di scorrimento (tracking)

scuri a scandole (shutter of strips)

Serramenti per scuri – hardware for shutters

fermascure (shutter catches)

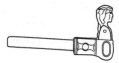

spagnoletta (shutter fastener) fixed to outer leaf

handle, also secures inner leaf

bolt into bottom of frame

Gli scuri e le serrande avvolgibili - shutters

bandella di cerniera (f)	strap of hinge
battente (m)	leaf, single shutter
cassonetto coprirullo (m)	casing for roller shutter
catenaccio (m)	latch
cerniera (f)	hinge
fermascuri (m)	shutter catch
guide di scorrimento (f)	tracking on roller shutters
persiana (f)	slatted shutter
scuri a scandole (m)	shutter of strips
scuri a scandole trasversali	wooden shutter with cross bars
scuri con cerniere a bandella	shutter with strap hinges
serranda avvolgibile	roller shutters
serratura di finestra (f)	window lock
stecca trasversale (f)	diagonal brace on shutter
spagnoletta (f)	shutter fastening

Le scale – staircases

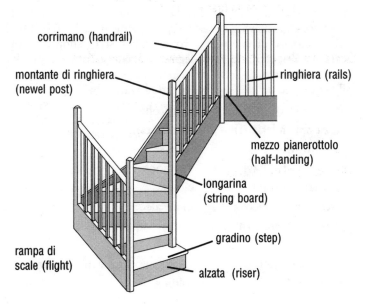

corrimano (handrail)

montante di ringhiera (newel post)

ringhiera (rails)

mezzo pianerottolo (half-landing)

longarina (string board)

gradino (step)

rampa di scale (flight)

alzata (riser)

alzata (f)	riser
corrimano (m)	handrail
gradino (m)	step
longarina (f)	string board
mezzo pianerottolo (m)	half-landing
montante di ringhiera (m)	pilaster, newel post
pedata (f)	tread
rampa di scale (f)	flight
ringhiera (m)	rails
scala (f)	staircase
scala a pioli	step ladder
scala a chiocciola	spiral staircase
scala pieghevole	fold-away stairs, e.g. for loft
scala a chiocciola	spiral staircase

Armadi e mensole – cupboards and shelves

For most of us, making built-in cupboards and shelves isn't a *falegnameria* job – we just head for the nearest IKEA and buy flat-packs and shelving systems. It's the same in Italy. You'll find IKEA there, but if you want proper Italian style, shop with the locals like Bricofer and Puntolegno. You could, for example, kit out your *camera da letto principale* (master bedroom) with a fully equipped *armadio a muro* (fitted wardrobe).

armadio (m)	wardrobe
barra appenderia (f)	clothes rail
cassetto (m)	drawer
gancio portachiavi	key hook
guardaroba (m)	closet
inserito in un'alcova	in an alcove
pannello laterale (m)	side of cupboard
mensola (f)	shelf
porte scorrevoli	sliding doors for cupboard or room
porte pieghevoli	folding doors

L'armadio a muro – fitted wardrobe
(Typical elements in a flat-pack kit)

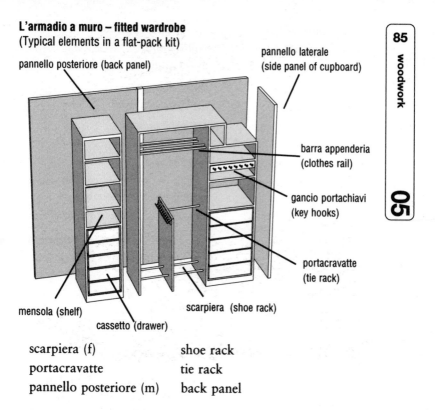

pannello posteriore (back panel)

pannello laterale
(side panel of cupboard)

barra appenderia
(clothes rail)

gancio portachiavi
(key hooks)

portacravatte
(tie rack)

mensola (shelf)

cassetto (drawer)

scarpiera (shoe rack)

scarpiera (f)	shoe rack
portacravatte	tie rack
pannello posteriore (m)	back panel

Il legno – wood

The wood section of a Italian *negozio di Fai-da-Te* looks much
the same as one in any UK DIY store. If you want solid wood,
ask for *legno massiccio*, as opposed to some form of *pannello*
(manufactured panel).

bordatura (f)	beading
betulla (f)	beech
castagno (m)	chestnut
compensato (m)	plywood
… impiallicciato	plywood with veneer
con bordi maschio e femmina	tongue and grooved (literally, 'with masculine and femine edges')
legno (m) duro	hardwood

legno duro tropicale	tropical hardwood
legno massiccio	solid wood
legno tenero	softwood
MDF	MDF
melaminato	melamine-coated
pannello (m)	panel
… in legno	wood panel
… di fibre compresse	hardboard
… truciolato rivestito in melamina	melamine surfaced chipboard panel, e.g. Contiboard
… truciolato impiallicciato	veneered chipboard panel
… decorativo	veneer
pino (m)	pine
quercia (f)	oak
truciolato (m)	chipboard

Gli attrezzi – tools

If you are going to do any *negozio di Fai-da-Te* (DIY), you will need *gli attrezzi* (some tools) and *cassetta degli attrezzi* (a toolbox) – or even *un garage* (a workshop) – to keep them in. Here's an assortment of tools that you may find useful.

accetta (f)	axe
cacciavite (m)	screwdriver
cacciavite elettrico (m)	electric screwdriver
calibro (m)	mortice gauge
carta (f) abrasiva	abrasive paper
carta vetrata (f)	sandpaper
chiodo (m)	nail
chiave (f)	spanner
chiave universale	adjustable spanner
chiave a brugola	allen key
colla per legno (f)	wood glue
forbici (f)	scissors

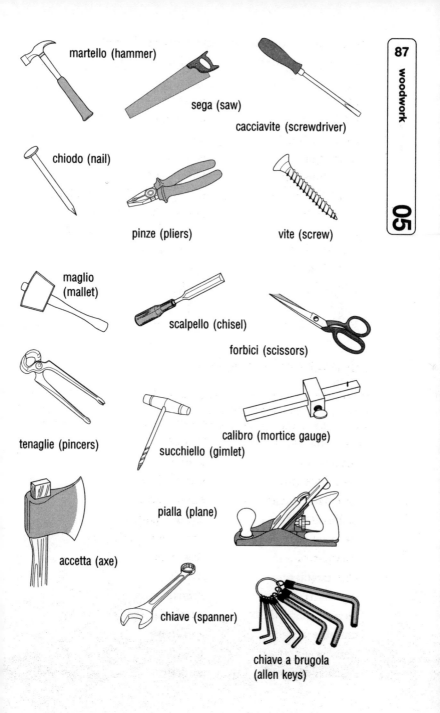

martello (hammer)

sega (saw)

cacciavite (screwdriver)

chiodo (nail)

pinze (pliers)

vite (screw)

maglio (mallet)

scalpello (chisel)

forbici (scissors)

tenaglie (pincers)

succhiello (gimlet)

calibro (mortice gauge)

accetta (axe)

pialla (plane)

chiave (spanner)

chiave a brugola (allen keys)

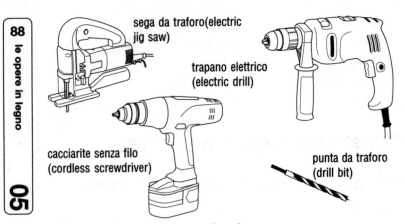

sega da traforo (electric jig saw)

trapano elettrico
(electric drill)

cacciarite senza filo
(cordless screwdriver)

punta da traforo
(drill bit)

falsa squadra	bevel square
girabacchino (m)	brace, of bit and brace
levigatrice (f)	sander
maglio (m)	mallet
martello (m)	hammer
metro pieghevole (m)	folding rule
metro a nastro	tape measure
pialla (f)	plane
pinze (f)	pliers
pistola graffettatrice (f)	staple gun
punta da trapano (f)	drill bit
punteruolo (m)	bradawl
raspa (f)	rasp
righello metallico (m)	metal rule
scalpello (m)	mortice chisel
scalpello per legno	wood chisel
sega (f)	saw
sega circolare	circular saw
sega da traforo	electric jig saw
serie di chiavi (f)	set of spanners
squadra	set square
squadra a T (f)	T-square
succhiello (m)	gimlet

taglierino (m)	cutter (Stanley knife)
tagliavetro (m)	glass cutter
tenaglie (f)	pincers
trapano elettrico (m)	electric drill
vite (f)	screw

English–Italian quick reference

Internal woodwork – le opere in legno interne

cupboard	credenza (f)
false ceiling	controsoffitto (m)
floor	pavimento (m)
floorboard	asse (f) del pavimento
frame, door or window	telaio (m)
joist	travicello (m)
picture rail	cimasa (f)
pannelling	pannellatura (f)
shelf	mensola (m)
skirting board	battiscopa (m)
wood flooring	pavimento in legno (m)

Doors – le porte

beading for glass	bordatura (f)
door	porta (f)
door frame	telaio (m)
door knob	pomello (m)
doorstep	soglia (f)
fanlight	lunetta (f)
letter box	cassetta delle lettere (f)
sliding door	porta scorrevole
swing door	porta a vento

Hardware for doors – serramenti per porte

bolt	chiavistello (m)
catch	fermo (m)
cylinder lock	serratura a cilindro (f)
deadlock	serratura da infilare con e senza scrocco
door handle	maniglia (f)
hinge	cerniera (f)
hinge, split	cerniera estraibile (f)
key	chiave (f)
keyhole	buco della serratura (m)
spyhole for door	spioncino (m)
mortice lock	serratura da infilare

Windows – le finestre

bay window	finestra a bovindo (f)
casement window	finestra a battente
double glazing	doppi vetri
french window	porta-finestra (f)
glass	vetro (m)
leaf or light	luce (f)
lintel	architrave (f)
pane	vetro (m)
mosquito nets	zanzariere
skylight	finestra a lucernaio
window pane	vetro (m)
window frame	telaio (m)
windowsill	davanzale (m)

Shutters – gli scuri

hinge	cerniera (m)
latch	catenaccio (m)
roller shutter	serranda avvolgibile (f)
roller shutter casing	cassonetto coprirullo (m)

shutter, slatted	persiana (f)
shutter with cross bars	scuro a scandole trasversali
shutter with strap hinges	scuro con cerniere a bandella
shutter catch	fermascuri (m)
shutter fastening	spagnoletta (f)
strap hinge	cerniera a bandella (f)
window lock	serratura (f)

Staircases – le scale

ladder	scala (f)
rails	ringhiera (f)
flight of steps	rampa (f)
fold-away stairs	scala pieghevole
half-landing	mezzo pianerottolo (m)
handrail	corrimano (m)
newel post	montante di ringhiera (m)
riser	alzata (f)
spiral staircase	scala a chiocciola
staircase	scala (f)
step ladder	scala a pioli (f)
step	gradino (f)

Cupboards and shelves – armadi e mensole

clothes rail	barra appenderia (f)
drawer	cassetto (m)
fitted wardrobe	guardaroba (m)
doors, folding	porte pieghevoli
doors, sliding	porte scorrevoli
key hook	gancio portachiavi
shelf	mensola (f)
shelves, set of	serie di mensole (f)
shoe rack	scarpiera (f)
tie rack	portacravatte (m)
wardrobe	armadio (m)

Wood – il legno

beading	bordatura (f)
beech	betulla (f)
chestnut	castagno (m)
chipboard	truciolato (m)
hardboard	pannello di fibre compresse
hardwod	legno duro
MDF	MDF
melamine panel	pannello rivestito in melamina
oak	quercia (f)
pine	pino (m)
veneer (m)	pialliccio decorativo (f)
plywood	compensato (m)
softwood	legno tenero
solid wood	legno massiccio
tongue and grooved	con bordi maschio e femmina
veneered panel	pannello impiallicciato
wood panel	pannello in legno

Tools – gli utensili

allen key	chiave a brugola (f)
axe	accetta (f)
bevel square	falsa squadra (f)
brace, of bit and brace	girabacchino (m)
chisel	scalpello (m)
cutter (Stanley knife)	taglierino (m)
drill bit	punta da trapano (f)
electric drill	trapano elettrico (m)
electric jig saw	sega da traforo (f)
electric screwdriver	cacciavite elettrico (m)
folding rule	righello pieghevole (m)
gimlet	succhiello (m)
glass cutter	tagliavetro (m)

hammer	martello (m)
mallet	maglio (m)
metal rule	righello metallico (m)
nail	chiodo (m)
plane	pialla (f)
pincers	tenaglie (f)
pliers	pinze (f)
rasp	raspa (f)
sander	levigatrice (f)
sandpaper	carta vetrata (f)
saw	sega (f)
saw, circular	sega circolare
scissors	forbici (f)
screw	vite (f)
screwdriver	cacciavite (m)
set square	squadra (f)
spanner	chiave (f)
spanner, adjustable	chiave universale
spanners, set of	serie di chiavi (f)
staple gun	pistola graffettatrice (f)
T-square	squadra a T (f)
tape measure	metro a nastro (m)
wood glue	colla per legno (f)

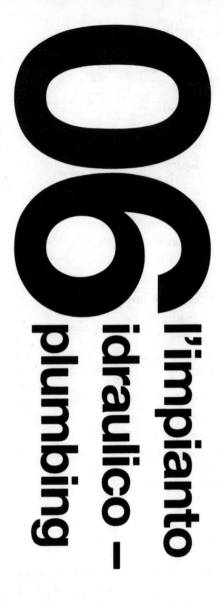

06

l'impianto
idraulico –
plumbing

Almost the same...

The days of 'Napoleon's footsteps' loos are long gone – although there are still some in the odd bar or railway station – so that now plumbing systems look much the same in Italy and the UK. There are a few visible differences – bathrooms are usually fully tiled, and the washbasins typically have plunger-valves not plugs. The important differences, as you'd expect, are not so visible.

Italian pipe and fitting sizes are metric – just as UK sizes are metric, but Italian sizes are properly metric while UK sizes are just conversions of the old Imperial measures. So, in the UK you have 15mm ($^5/_8$"), 19mm ($^3/_4$"inch), 22mm ($^7/_8$") and the like, while the Italian sizes are 10mm, 12mm, 16mm, 20mm, etc. The upshot is that you cannot normally use British fittings in a Italian plumbing system. Those lovely taps that you saw in Debenhams won't fit on your bath.

The second point you need to note is Italian houses have a direct cold water supply system – there's no cold tank. That'll give you a bit more space in the attic, but the important things in plumbing terms are that your water supply is at mains pressure, and that this is higher than you get in the UK. (If you have ever been flattened against the side in an Italian shower you'll know this.) In the UK, mains pressure is typically 0.5 bar or less and at most 1 bar. In Italy, pressure of 3 or 4 bars is normal. If the pressure is so high in your area that it is a problem, you can fit a regolatore (regulator) to reduce it to a more reasonable level.

Water is supplied by private companies and is metered, with prices varying slightly from area to area. If your house is not on the main drains your water costs should be lower as there are no sewerage charges.

Check at the comune

♦ In some areas, you may have to fit a *valovola d'isolamento* (isolating valve) to prevent your domestic system flowing back into the mains and polluting the supply. Your water company will tell you if you need one.

♦ If you need to install *una fossa biologica* (septic tank) you must get your plans approved at the *comune*.

Le tubazioni – pipework

With modern materials and fixings, plumbing can be a job for an amateur – but even if you are not doing the plumbing yourself, it is helpful to know what the professionals are on about, and what you are paying for.

L'alimentazione idrica – supply

The water supply pipework is normally copper, though flexible braided polyethylene is increasing used. On copper pipes, the connections may be *saldate* (soldered) or *filettata* (threaded, i.e. compression).

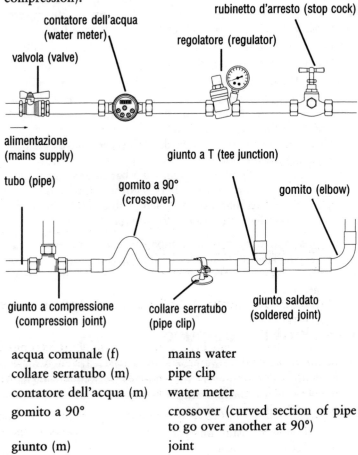

rubinetto d'arresto (stop cock)

contatore dell'acqua
(water meter)

regolatore (regulator)

valvola (valve)

alimentazione
(mains supply)

giunto a T (tee junction)

tubo (pipe)

gomito a 90°
(crossover)

gomito (elbow)

giunto a compressione
(compression joint)

collare serratubo
(pipe clip)

giunto saldato
(soldered joint)

acqua comunale (f)	mains water
collare serratubo (m)	pipe clip
contatore dell'acqua (m)	water meter
gomito a 90°	crossover (curved section of pipe to go over another at 90°)
giunto (m)	joint

giunto ad angolo	angle joint
giunto a compressione	compression joint
giunto a T (m)	tee junction
giunto di riduzione	reducing joint
giunto saldato	soldered joint
manicotto (m)	sleeve
regolatore (m)	regulator – only needed where high pressure is a problem
piombo (m)	lead
plastica	plastic
PVC	PVC
rame (m)	copper
rame flessibile	flexible copper, sold in rolls
riduttore (m) di pressione	pressure reducer
rubinetto (m)	tap
rubinetto d'arresto	stop cock
rubinetto di scarico	drain cock
tubo (m)	pipe, length of piping
tubazione (f)	pipework
tubi diritti (m)	straight pipes
tubi flessibili	braided polyethylene – flexible pipes often used to connect sink and bath taps to the fixed pipes
valvola di isolamento (f)	isolating valve
valvola a saracinesca (f)	valve, sluice gate

L'impianto di scarico delle acque – waste water system

There are two systems here: *i tubi di grondaia* (guttering) for *l'acqua piovana* (rain water) and the internal system for *le acque domestiche* ('domestic waters', from sinks and baths) and *le acque reflue* ('sluice waters', from the toilets).

Guttering can be installed by a builder – galivanised, i.e. zinc-coated, iron was commonly used for guttering, though most is now PVC.

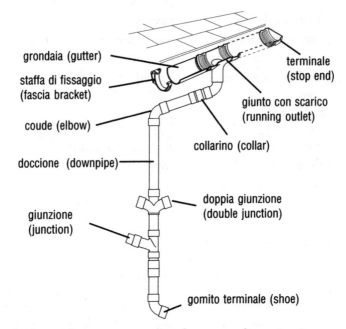

grondaia (gutter)

staffa di fissaggio (fascia bracket)

coude (elbow)

doccione (downpipe)

giunzione (junction)

terminale (stop end)

giunto con scarico (running outlet)

collarino (collar)

doppia giunzione (double junction)

gomito terminale (shoe)

For the internal systems, carrying *le acque di scarico* ('waste water', i.e. all household water from sinks, baths and toilets), you need an *idraulico* (plumber).

There may be separate mains drains for rainwater and waste water, and you must connect properly.

acqua di scarico	waste water
acque domestiche	domestic waters
acqua piovana (f)	rain water
acque reflue	sluice waters
cemento-amianto (m)	asbestos cement – once used for drains, this is a health hazard
collarino (m)	collar, coupler
doccione (m)	downpipe
doppia giunzione	double junction
ghisa (f)	cast iron
giunto (m)	joint
giunto con scarico (m)	running outlet, joins gutter to down pipe

giunzione (f)	junction
gomito terminale (m)	shoe – the outlet spout at bottom of the down pipe
gres (m)	stoneware – commonly used for drains in the past
grondaia (f)	gutter
staffa di fissaggio (f)	fascia bracket
terminale (m)	stop end for gutter
tubi di scarico (f)	waste pipes
tubo di troppo-pieno	overflow
zincato	zinc-coated, galvanised

Il bagno – the bathroom

If you want a typical Italian bathroom, you need lots of tiles – ceramic tiles on the floor and right up the walls. Tiles mean lower maintenance and easier cleaning, and cold-to-stand-on after-a-hot-bath is not the same problem in the warmer climate.

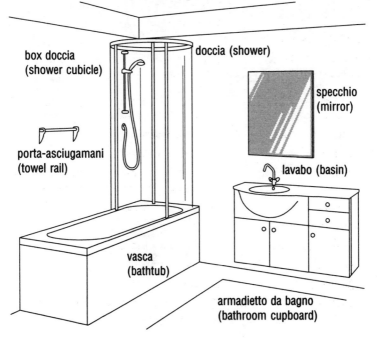

box doccia (shower cubicle)

doccia (shower)

specchio (mirror)

porta-asciugamani (towel rail)

lavabo (basin)

vasca (bathtub)

armadietto da bagno (bathroom cupboard)

As an alternative to an ordinary shower, you can have a hydromassage – one with horizontal jets that can pound you from the side. You can get self-contained *cabine idromassaggio* (hydro-massage cubicles), or fit a *colonna idromassaggio* (hydromassage column) instead of an ordinary shower head – just make sure that your cubicle is watertight!

Una colonna idromassaggio

Il lavabo - the basin

Mixer taps and lever operated plughole covers are the norm for basins and baths.

Il lavabo

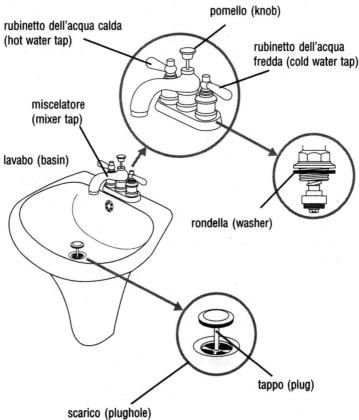

pomello (knob)

rubinetto dell'acqua calda
(hot water tap)

rubinetto dell'acqua
fredda (cold water tap)

miscelatore
(mixer tap)

lavabo (basin)

rondella (washer)

tappo (plug)

scarico (plughole)

There are two sorts of mixer taps: *un miscelatore monoblocco* has separate hot and cold controls; *un miscelatore monocomando* has a single lever which controls the volume and temperature.

miscelatore
monoblocco

miscelatore
monocomando

Il WC – the loo

It's one of those ironies of language that the Italians call the loo WC, from Water Closet. The technology is the same, though they seem to prefer the button flush mechanisms.

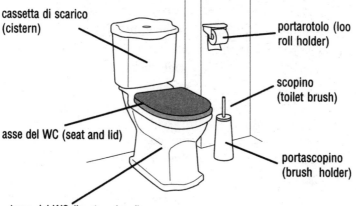

cassetta di scarico
(cistern)

portarotolo (loo
roll holder)

scopino
(toilet brush)

asse del WC (seat and lid)

portascopino
(brush holder)

tazza del WC (lavatory bowl)

Lexicon: il bagno – bathroom

addolcitore d'acqua (m)   water softening system
anello porta-asciugamani   towel ring
armadietto (m) da bagno   bathroom cabinet
armadietto dei medicinali   medicine cabinet
armadietto sopra WC   cupboard behind/over WC
asse del WC (f)   WC seat lid
attrezzature sanitarie (m)   fittings

bidet (m)	bidet
box doccia (m)	shower cubicle
carabottino (m)	duckboard/grating for stepping on after bath
cassetta di scarico (f)	WC cistern
cestino (m) a pedale	pedal bin
cestino dell'immondizia	rubbish bin
doccia (f)	shower
gancio (m)	hook
gancio porta-asciugamani	towel hook
idromassaggio (m)	hydromassage cabinet/system
idromassaggio (m)	hydromassaging
idrosanitari (m)	sanitary ware
lavabo (m)	basin
meccanismo di cacciata	flushing mechanism
mensola per doccia (f)	shower tidy
mensolina (f)	small shelf
miscelatore (m)	mixer tap
... monoblocco	... with separate controls
... monocomando	... with combine volume/temperature control
parete doccia (f)	shower screen
pesa-persone (m)	scales
piatto per doccia (m)	shower tray
pomello (m)	knob
porta-asciugamani (f)	towel rail
portabiancheria	laundry basket
portabicchiere (m)	toothmug holder
portarotolo (m)	loo roll holder
portasapone (m)	soap dish
portascopino (m)	brush and holder
rondella (f)	washer
rubinetto (m)	tap
dell'acqua calda	hot water tap

dell'acqua fredda	cold water tap
scaldasalviette (m)	heated towel rail
sifone (m) a bottiglia	bottle trap
sifone a ghiera	threaded 'ring' trap
sifone a S	S-bend
sifone a U	U-bend
scaldabagno (m)	water heater
scopino (m)	toilet brush
specchio (m)	mirror
tappo (m)	plug
tazza del WC (f)	toilet pan
tubo di scarico (m)	waste pipes, from basin or bath
vasca (f)	bathtub

La cucina - kitchen

I suspect that the main difference between the average kitchens in Italy and the UK is in the quality of the food – which is one of the reasons why we love Italy, isn't it? The appliances and fittings are much the same.

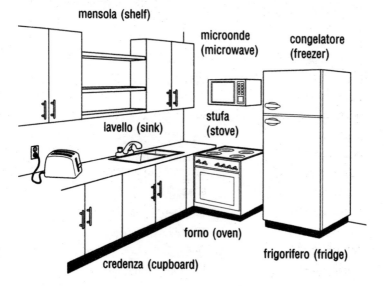

Il lavello – the sink

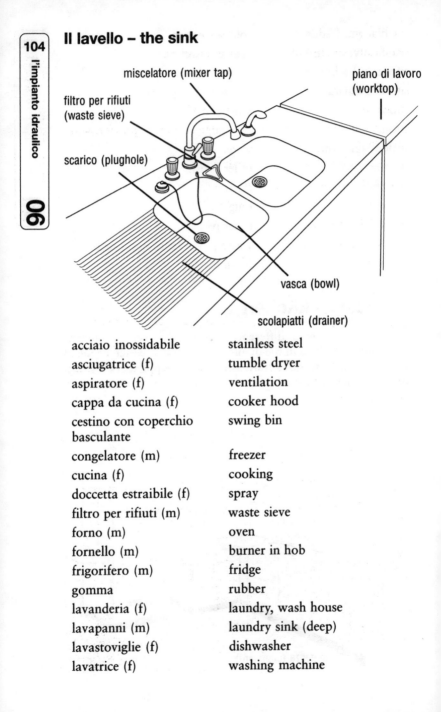

miscelatore (mixer tap)

piano di lavoro (worktop)

filtro per rifiuti (waste sieve)

scarico (plughole)

vasca (bowl)

scolapiatti (drainer)

acciaio inossidabile	stainless steel
asciugatrice (f)	tumble dryer
aspiratore (f)	ventilation
cappa da cucina (f)	cooker hood
cestino con coperchio basculante	swing bin
congelatore (m)	freezer
cucina (f)	cooking
doccetta estraibile (f)	spray
filtro per rifiuti (m)	waste sieve
forno (m)	oven
fornello (m)	burner in hob
frigorifero (m)	fridge
gomma	rubber
lavanderia (f)	laundry, wash house
lavapanni (m)	laundry sink (deep)
lavastoviglie (f)	dishwasher
lavatrice (f)	washing machine

lavello (m)	kitchen sink
lavello autonomo (m)	stand-alone sink
microonde (f)	microwave
piano (m) di cottura	hob
piano di lavoro	work surface
piano laminato con bordi arrotondati	roll edge laminate (postformed)
piletta automatica (f)	sink plunger
troppopieno (m)	overflow
scarico (m)	plughole
scolapiatti del lavello (m)	drainer
stufa (f)	stove
tappo (m)	plug
vasca del lavello (m)	bowl

La fossa biologica – the septic tank

If your house is not connected to the *rete fognaria pubblica* (mains drains), then you are going to need *una fossa biologica* (septic tank – or a *microstazione di depurazione* (purification microstation). If you have an old *fossa*, you may well need a new one – or a microstation.

But first, what is a *fossa biologica*? They vary, but essentially a *fossa* is a system of chambers, dug in the ground near the house.

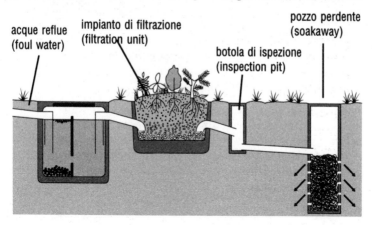

acque reflue
(foul water)

impianto di filtrazione
(filtration unit)

pozzo perdente
(soakaway)

botola di ispezione
(inspection pit)

The first chamber is a watertight tank into which the sewer and house drains empty foul water. Solid matter is broken down by bacteriological action – a process which takes around a week. Not all solid matter breaks down, which is why you must call out the *addetto allo svuotamento* (septic tank emptier) every three or four years.

The second chamber is the filtration unit, typically a bed of sand. This may be closed, or capped with earth with grass or small plants growing above. (Trees and bushes must be kept away from *fossas* because their roots can damage the structures.

The final chamber is the *pozzo perdente* (soakaway) – a porous pit filled with rubble or gravel. The filtration unit and soakaway can be combined into one, or if the filtered water can be released into a stream, the soakaway may not be necessary.

A *fossa* system takes some space – a minimum of 150m² of free from trees and shrubs. If there isn't that much free space, then there is an alternative – *la microstazione di depurazione* (purification microstation). This is a motorised system that circulates and aerates the water, to break down solids faster. Because it is faster, less storage volume is needed, and as it has its own filtration system, the whole structure is far more compact.

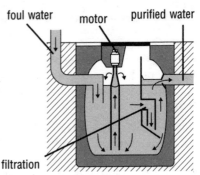

foul water   motor   purified water

filtration

The *fossa* system may also have a separate grease trap, where grease, oil and other floating nasties will collect at the top, and must be removed periodically. The grease trap may be integral to the *fossa* – but the floating gunge still needs removal.

A new *fossa* must meet stringent standards on water quality, and cannot be constructed without a *permesso di scarico delle acque* (permit to allow water to drain). These are issued by the *comune*, which is where you must start. Their expert will advise on how large a *fossa* you need and where – and if – it can be located on your land.

The simplest solution is probably to put the whole business in the hands of a *fossa* building firm. They will know the ropes, and you'll have to hire them anyway unless you want to dig those holes yourself and manhandle the tanks into place! The cost of getting them to deal with the bureaucracy will be small in comparison to the cost of the installation. Depending upon the size of the *fossa*, the nature of the land and other factors, this should be in the region of €5,000 to €10,000.

06

The fossa way

Fossas and micro-stations are organic systems that are designed for dealing with organic matter. They cannot cope with cigarette ends, tampons, *preservativi* (condoms) and other indigestible objects that people routinely flush down the toilet. Bleach, paint, white spirit, and other harsh chemicals cannot be flushed either, as these will kill the bacteria that make the *fossa* work. Ordinary soap is not a problem, and there are washing powders and cleaners that are safe for use with *fossa* systems.

Look after your *fossa* and your *fossa* will look after you!

---

acque reflue	foul water
addetto allo svuotamento della fossa biologica	septic tank emptier
botola di ispezione (f)	inspection pit
fossa biologica (f)	septic tank
impianto di filtrazione (f)	filtration unit
liquame (m)	sewage
permesso (m) di scarico delle acque	permit to drain water from land
pozzo perdente (m)	soakaway
purificazione (f)	purification
tubo di caduta (m)	soil pipe

Gli attrezzi – tools

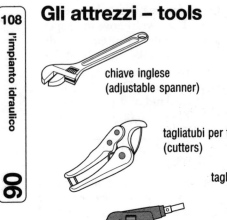

chiave inglese
(adjustable spanner)

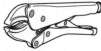

pinze a morsa (mole grip)

tagliatubi per tubi in PVC
(cutters)

tagliatubi (pipe cutter)

cannello per saldare (soldering lamp)

cannello (m)	blow lamp
chiave per dadi (f)	spanner
chiave inglese	adjustable spanner
tagliatubi (m)	pipe cutter
cannello per saldare (m)	soldering lamp
pinze a morsa (f)	mole grip, wrench
seghetto (m)	hacksaw
tagliatubi per tubi in PVC	cutters (for PVC pipes)
borsa d'idraulico (f)	plumber's bag, usually soft leather
piletta automatica (f)	plunger

The essential plumbing term

When you need this, you won't have time to learn it, so learn it now.

'*Aiuto, c'è una perdita!*' (Help, there's a leak).

English-Italian quick reference

Piperwork – le tubazioni

asbetos cement	cemento-amianto
cast iron	ghisa (f)
copper	rame (m)
downpipe	doccione (m)
drain cock	rubinetto di scarico (m)
elbow joint	gomito (m)
galvanised	zincato
gutter	grondaia (f)
joint	giunto (m)
soldered	saldato
compression	a compressione
junction	giunzione (f)
lead	piombo (m)
mains water	acqua comunale
pipe	tubo (m)
pipe clip	collare serratubo (m)
plastic	plastica (f)
regulator	regolatore (m)
stoneware	gres (m)
stop cock	rubinetto d'arresto
valve	valvola a saracinesca (f)
waste water system	impianto di scarico delle acque
water meter	contatore dell'acqua (m)

Bathroom – il bagno

basin	lavabo (m)
bathtub	vasca (f)
cistern	cassetta di scarco
hydromassage cabinet	idromassaggio (m)
laundry basket	portabiancheria (f)
medicine cabinet	armadietto dei medicinali (m)

mirror	specchio (m)
mixer tap	miscelatore (m)
plug	tappo (f)
rubbish bin	cestino dell'immondizia (m)
sanitary ware	idrosanitari
scales	pesapersone (m)
shower	doccia (f)
shower cubicle	box doccia
soap dish	portasapone (m)
tap	rubinetto (m)
toilet brush	scopino (m)
toilet pan	tazza del WC (f)
toilet roll holder	portarotolo (m)
toothbrush holder	portabicchiere (m)
towel rail	porta-asciugamani (m)
towel rail, heated	scaldasalviette (m)
U-bend	sifone (m)
washer	rondella (f)
waste pipes	tubi di scarico (m)
WC seat lid	asse del WC (m)

Kitchen – la cucina

bowl	vaschetta (f)
burner in hob	fornello (m)
cooker hood	cappa di cucina (f)
dishwasher	lavapiatti (f)
drainer	sgocciolatoio (m)
freezer	congelatore (m)
fridge	refrigeratore (m)
hob	piastra da cucina (f)
kitchen sink	lavello (m)
microwave	microonde (m)
oven	forno (m)
overflow	troppopieno (m)

plug (hole)	tappo/scarico (f)
rubber	gomma
sink plunger	piletta automatica (f)
spray	doccetta estraibile (f)
stainless steel	acciaio inossidabile
stove	stufa (f)
swing bin	cestino (m) con coperchio basculante
tumble dryer	asciugatrice (f)
washing machine	lavatrice (f)
work surface	piano di lavoro (m)
waste sieve	filtro per rifiuti (m)

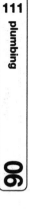

Septic tank – la fossa biologica

filtration unit	impianto di filtrazione (m)
foul water	acque reflue
inspection pit	botola d'ispezione (f)
purification	purificazione (f)
septic tank	fossa biologica (f)
sewage	liquame
soakaway	pozzo perdente (m)
soil pipe	tubo di caduta (m)
septic tank emptier	addetto allo svuotamento delle fosse settiche (m)

Tools – gli attrezzi

adjustable spanner	chiave inglese (f)
blow lamp	cannello (m)
cutters (for PVC pipes)	tagliatubi (per tubi in PVC)
hacksaw	seghetto
mole grip	pinze a morsa (f)
pipe cutter	tagliatubi (m)
plumber's bag	borsa d'idraulico (f)
soldering lamp	cannello per saldare (m)
spanner	chiave (f)

07

il riscaldamento e l'elettricità – heating and electricity

Almost the same...

Heating and lighting appliances and usages are actually very similar in the UK and Italy. If many of us feel that things are different, it is probably because we are comparing UK town life with Italian rural life.

With electricity, the most obvious difference is that in Italy there are several levels of power supply. Like us they have a plethora of tariffs, but all theirs are offered by one firm instead of a mass of competing firms. Power supply is less reliable than in the UK, especially in rural areas, mainly because it's all carried by overhead cables rather than underground ones and because of the extreme weather conditions. Thunderstorms are a common cause of disruption – and of damage. You must turn off TVs and computers during storms, and disconnect aerials. You should also install surge protection and UPS (uninterruptible power supply) if you use a computer for work.

With gas, there is a more widespread use of bottled or tank gas as piped gas does not extend to the most rural and mountainous areas.

Wood is used more as a fuel. Supplies are plentiful, prices are competitive and rural houses generally have the space to store large stocks.

Il riscaldamento – heating

The first question is, which fuel(s) will you use? You have quite a choice:

* *la legna* (wood) is very popular in mountainous and rural areas, where wood-burning stoves or fires are still very common, often alongside central heating. It is bought by the *metro cubo* (cubic metre), and must be stored for at least a few months before it is needed – green wood produces a lot of tar which condenses in the chimney and creates problems.

* *il carbone* (coal) is rarely used as Italy is not a coal-producing country.

* *il gasolio* (oil) is widely used for running central heating systems in all areas. The cost varies with the price of crude oil.

- *il gas* (gas) comes in three varieties: *gas di rete* (town gas), supplied by ENEL, and propane or butane stored, like fuel oil, in a large *serbatoio* (tank) above the ground or bought in *bombole* (bottles).

- *l'elettricità* (electricity) is more expensive in Italy than in the UK, and not a very economic choice for heating.

What is right for you will depend upon the nature of your house and the way that you intend to use it.

- Is there *un caminetto* (fireplace) or can one be installed?

- If the house is in an urban area, are there restrictions on solid fuel fires?

- How much space do you have for wood storage or for an oil or gas tank?

- If the house is not connected to mains gas, can it be connected, and at what cost?

- Will the house be used mainly in the summer, or at times throughout the year, or will it be your permanent home? If you only need the occasional heating on chilly evenings, the cost and efficiency of the fuel is a minor consideration.

Il riscaldamento centrale – central heating

Il riscaldamento ad acqua (heating by water) generally works by means of *radiatori*, though *il riscaldamento a pavimento* (underfloor heating) is a possible alternative.

A modern Italian system is well regulated. A *sonda esterna* (external sensor) picks up the outside temperature and adjusts the temperature of the circulating water appropriately. Within the house, a *termostato di zona* (area thermostat) will control the heat in a zone or room, while a *valvola termostatica* (radiator thermostat) can control individual radiators.

The *caldaia* (boiler) can be a *muro* (wall-mounted) or *autoportante* (free-standing).

Il riscaldamento centrale

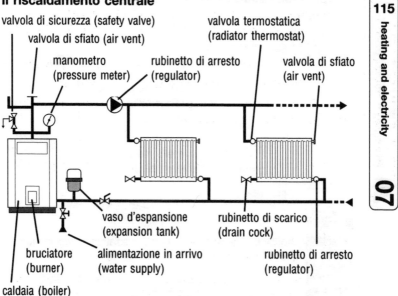

valvola di sicurezza (safety valve)
valvola di sfiato (air vent)
manometro (pressure meter)
rubinetto di arresto (regulator)
valvola termostatica (radiator thermostat)
valvola di sfiato (air vent)
vaso d'espansione (expansion tank)
rubinetto di scarico (drain cock)
bruciatore (burner)
alimentazione in arrivo (water supply)
rubinetto di arresto (regulator)
caldaia (boiler)

Il caminetto – the fireplace

An open fire is always attractive, though carrying in the logs and clearing out the ash can become a chore if you have to do it regularly.

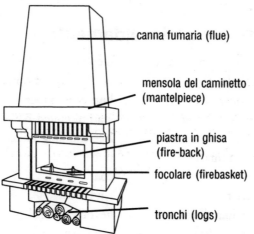

canna fumaria (flue)
mensola del caminetto (mantelpiece)
piastra in ghisa (fire-back)
focolare (firebasket)
tronchi (logs)

Caminetti can be rather grand, built from thick stone and heavy beams

Le apparecchiature di riscaldamento – heating equipment

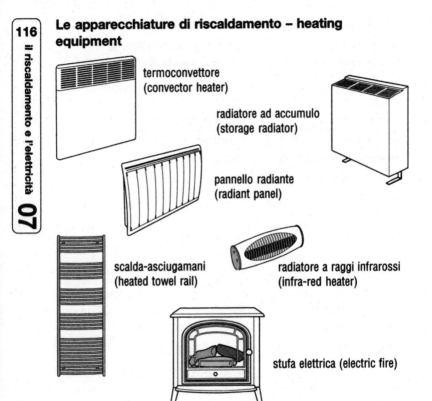

termoconvettore
(convector heater)

radiatore ad accumulo
(storage radiator)

pannello radiante
(radiant panel)

scalda-asciugamani
(heated towel rail)

radiatore a raggi infrarossi
(infra-red heater)

stufa elettrica (electric fire)

Lexicon: il riscaldamento – heating

alimentazione in arrivo (f)	incoming water supply
bombola (f)	bottle, e.g. for butane
bruciatore (m)	burner in boiler
caldaia (f) a muro	wall-mounted boiler
caldaia autoportante	free-standing boiler
canna fumaria	flue
carbone (m)	coal
ceneriera (f)	cinder tray
centralina di controllo (f)	heating controls
elettricità (f)	electricity

focolare (m)	firebasket
gas di rete	town gas
gas metano	methane gas
gasolio (m)	heating oil
legna (f)	wood
manometro (m)	pressure meter
mensola del caminetto (f)	mantlepiece
pannello radiante (m)	radiant panel
piastra in ghisa	fire-back
radiatore a raggi infrarossi	infra-red heater
radiatore ad accumulo	storage radiator
radiatore ad olio (m)	oil-filled radiator
riscaldamento (m)	heating
... ad aria calda	hot-air
... ad acqua	heating by water
rubinetto di arresto (m)	regulator/stopcock on radiator
rubinetto di scarico (m)	drain cock
scalda-asciugamani (m)	heated towel rail
serbatoio (m)	tank for oil or propane
sonda (f)	sensor
spazzacamino (m)	chimney sweep
stufa (f)	stove
stufa a legna	wood burning stove
... con canna fumaria	wood burning stove with flue
stufa elettrica	electric fire
tegolone di colmo (m)	chimney-flue tile
termoconvettore (m)	convector heater
termostato di zona	area thermostat
tronco (m)	log
valvola di sfiato (f)	air vent, at the highest point for venting a system, or on a radiator
valvola di sicurezza (f)	safety valve
valvola termostatica	radiator thermostat
vaso d'espansione (m)	expansion tank

Heating and lightning

If you have a fuel-oil or propane tank it must be earthed. Some friends, enjoying a dramatic thunderstorm one night, watched in horror as lightning struck their oil tank. It glowed bright blue, but fortunately nothing else happened! They had a lightning conductor fitted the next day. Their luck didn't hold though that night – another strike fried their TV, video, satellite box and most of the telephone wiring and sockets in the house.

L'alimentazione elettrica – the electricity supply

Monophase and triphase

In Italy, there are two distinct types of electricity supply. *Monofase* is the same as our domestic supply, though at 220 volts, instead of our 230 volts. *Trifase* provides both 220 and 380 volts supply and is mainly designed for industrial use. (*Trifase* is delivered down three live wires, instead of one, which is why the voltage can be higher.) It's what's usually supplied to farms to power their machinery, but if your house is in the countryside, it may be what is supplied to you.

In practice, having *trifase* doesn't create any problems, as normal domestic equipment can be run off it simply by selecting the 220 volt supply.

Wiring and rewiring

Note that rewiring tends to be more expensive than in the UK, though as with all work on a house, using a registered tradesman means that you have a guarantee of quality. You should employ a registered electrician to connect you to the mains.

The incoming electricity supply, up to the *contatore* (meter) and the *interruttore di rete* (mains switch), is the responsibility of ENEL.

Fusibili e interruttori di circuito – fuses and circuit breakers

A modern *scatola dei fusibili* (fuse box) doesn't have *fusibili* (fuses), but instead has an *interruttore di sicurezza* (cut-out) or an *interruttore di circuito* (circuit breaker) on each branch.

The best *interruttori di sicurezza* are the differential variety, which give greater protection against electric shocks. They have a normal magno-thermal cut-out which is triggered by a surge in the voltage or a short circuit, and a cut-out which responds to a change in the differential between the live and the neutral wires.

fusibile (fuse)

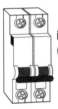

interruttore di circuito (circuit breaker)

interruttore differenziale (differential cut-out)

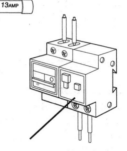

Sockets

The Italians use round-pin *prese di corrente* (electric sockets). There are two types: *bipolari* (2-pin) for lamps and *bipolari + terra* (2-pin + earth) for everything else. (The earth connects through a pin on the socket and a hole on the plug.)

UK 230 volt appliances will work perfectly well on Italian 220 volt supply – as long as you have plug adaptors – but it's usually best to buy Italian. You don't have the plug problem and it's easier to take it back if it doesn't work.

Telephone plugs and sockets are also different shapes to those in the UK, so buy your phones in Italy as well.

L'elettricità – electricity

alimentazione elettrica (f)	electrical supply
cavo (m)	cable
contatore (m)	meter
corrente (f) alterna	AC
corrente elettrica	electric current
corto circuito (m)	short circuit
far saltare i fusibili	blow the fuses
filo (m) di massa	earth (wire)
filo neutro	neutral wire
filo sotto tensione	live wire
fusibile (m)	fuse
fusibile a cartuccia	cartridge fuse
interruttore (m) di circuito	circuit breaker
interruttore di rete	mains switch
interruttore differenziale	differential cut-out
potenza (f)	power level
presa (f)	socket
presa bipolare + terra	2-pin + earth socket
spina (f)	plug
spina di terra	plug with earth pin
tensione (f)	voltage

Gli scaldabagni – water heaters

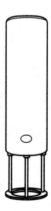

There are two main types of *scaldabagni* (water heaters): gas or electric on-demand boilers, which are all but identical to those in the UK, and the electric *serbatoi d'acqua calda* (hot-water tanks), which are different. These slim cylinders are wall-mounted or free-standing, depending on size, and almost always in white enamel. The heating element is normally of between 1kW and 2kW, which makes for relatively slow heating – typically 4 or 5 hours for a tankful.

Le apparecchiature elettriche – electrical appliances

Electrical appliances are all but the same in Italy and the UK – hardly surprising as they are largely from the same firms. You may have to hunt around a little to find a *bollitore* (kettle), as they are not regularly used by the Italians. Well, if you don't drink tea and you have a *caffettiera* and a *cavatappi* (cork screw), what's the point of a kettle?

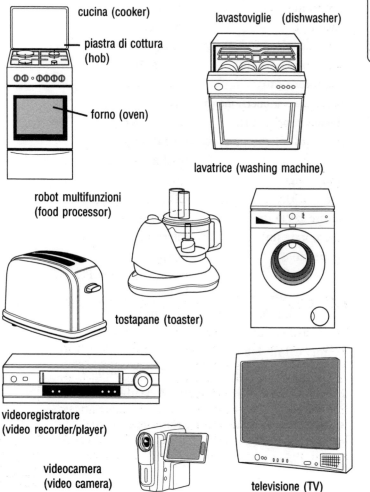

cucina (cooker)

piastra di cottura (hob)

forno (oven)

lavastoviglie (dishwasher)

lavatrice (washing machine)

robot multifunzioni (food processor)

tostapane (toaster)

videoregistratore (video recorder/player)

videocamera (video camera)

televisione (TV)

Le apparecchiature elettriche – electrical appliances

altoparlante (m)	speaker
amplificatore (m)	amplifier
asciugatrice (f)	tumble dryer
aspirapolvere (m)	vacuum cleaner
bollitore (m)	kettle
caffettiera (f)	coffee maker
computer (m)	computer
congelatore (m)	freezer
cucina (f)	cooker
ferro da stiro (m)	iron
forno incassato (m)	built-in oven
frigorifero (m)	refrigerator
frullatore a immersione (m)	hand-held mixer
guaina copricavi (f)	cable cover
impianto microfonico (m)	tape deck
lavatrice (m)	washing machine
lavastoviglie (m)	dishwasher
lettore CD	CD player
lettore DVD (m)	DVD player
microonde (m)	microwave
numerico/a	digital
PC (m)	micro computer, PC
piastra di cottura (f)	hob
robot multifunzioni (m)	food processor
scaldabagno (m)	water heater
scatola dei fusibili (f)	fuse box
segreteria telefonica (f)	answering machine
serbatoio (m) dell'acqua calda	hot water tank
sintonizzatore (m)	radio tuner
telefono (m)	telephone
televisione (f)	TV
... a schermo piatto	flat screen

... a schermo panoramico   widescreen TV
tostapane (m)   toaster
videocamera (f)   video camera
videoregistratore (m)   video recorder/player

Le apparecchiature d'illuminazione – light fittings

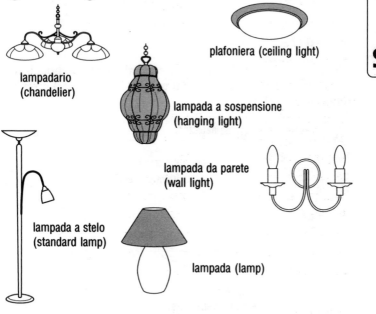

plafoniera (ceiling light)

lampadario
(chandelier)

lampada a sospensione
(hanging light)

lampada da parete
(wall light)

lampada a stelo
(standard lamp)

lampada (lamp)

alloggiamento (m)   light socket
faretto a parete (m)   spot light
illuminazione (f)   lighting
interruttore (m)   light switch
lampada (f)   lamp
lampada a sospensione   hangling light
lampada a stelo (m)   standard lamp
lampada alogena   halogen lamp
lampada da lettura   reading lamp

lampada da parete	wall light
lampada fluorescente	flourescent light
lampadario (m)	multi-bulb centre light, chandelier
lampadario a 4 luci	4-bulb centre light
lampadina (f)	light bulb
luce (f)	light
luce di lettura	reading light
plafoniera (f)	ceiling light

Gli attrezzi – tools

There are few special tools for electrical work – although they make electrician's versions of hammers, screwdrivers, knives and other tools.

rilevatore cavi (cable detector)

cacciavite provacircuiti
(screwdriver/current tester)

pinza spellafili
(wire cutters/strippers)

cacciavite (m) provacircuiti	voltage testing screwdriver
nastro isolante (m)	insulating tape
pinza amperometrica (f)	meter
rilevatore cavi (m)	cable detector
tagliafili/pinza (f) spellafili	wire cutters/strippers
tester (m) di corrente	current tester

L'energia solare – solar energy

In case you hadn't noticed, Italy is a sunnier country than the UK, and this makes solar energy more viable. *I pannelli solari* (solar panels) can provide 50% to 80% of a house's water heating needs, so an installation could more than pay for itself over time if you are there a significant part of the year. If the Italian house is your main residence, you may also be able to get a government grant towards the cost.

Le cellule fotovoltaiche (solar cells) for electricity generation may be worth investigating, depending on your power use.

English–Italian quick reference

Heating – il riscaldamento

air vent	valvola di sfiato (f)
boiler	caldaia (f)
central heating controls	centralina di controllo (f)
chimney sweep	spazzacamino (m)
cinder tray	ceneriera (f)
coal	carbone (m)
convector heater	termoconvettore (m)
electric fire	stufa elettrica (f)
firebasket	focolare (m)
flue	canna fumaria (f)
heated towel rail	scalda-asciugamani (m)
heating oil	gasolio (m)
infra-red heater	radiatore a raggi infrarossi (m)
log	tronco (m)
mantlepiece	mensola del caminetto (f)
radiator	radiatore (m)
radiator thermostat	valvola termostatica (f)
sensor	sonda (f)
storage radiator	radiatore ad accumulo

stove	stufa (f)
town gas	gas di rete
wood	legna (f)

Electricity – l'elettricità

AC	corrente alterna
blow the fuses	fare saltare i fusibili
circuit breaker	interruttore di circuito (m)
earth (wire)	terra (f)
electric current	corrente elettrica (f)
electrical supply	alimentazione elettrica (f)
fuse	fusibile (m)
fuse, cartridge	fusibile a cartuccia
fuse wire	filo fusibile (m)
live wire	filo sotto tensione
mains switch	interruttore di rete (m)
meter	contatore (m)
neutral wire	filo neutro (m)
plug	spina (f)
power level	potenza (f)
socket	presa (f)
short circuit	corto circuito (m)
voltage	tensione (f)

Electrical appliances – le apparecchiature elettriche

amplifier	amplificatore (m)
answering machine	segreteria telefonica (f)
cable cover	guaina copricavi (f)
CD player	lettore CD (m)
coffee maker	caffettiera (f)
computer	computer (m)
cooker	cucina (f)
digital	numerico/a
dishwasher	lavastoviglie (f)

DVD player	lettore DVD (m)
flat screen TV	televisione a schermo piatto
food processor	robot multifunzioni (m)
freezer	congelatore (m)
fridge	frigorifero (m)
fuse box	scatola dei fusibili (f)
hand-held mixer	frullatore ad immersione (m)
hob	piastra di cottura (f)
iron	ferro da stiro (m)
kettle	bollitore (m)
microwave	microonde (m)
oven	forno (m)
radio tuner	sintonizzatore (m)
speaker	altoparlante (m)
tape deck	impianto microfonico (m)
telephone	telefono (m)
toaster	tostapane (m)
tumble dryer	asciugatrice (f)
TV	televisione (f)
TV, widescreen	televisione a schermo panoramico
vacuum cleaner	aspirapolvere (f)
video camera	videocamera (f)
video recorder/player	videoregistratore (m)
washing machine	lavatrice (f)

Light fittings – le apparecchiature di illuminazione

ceiling light	plafoniera (f)
chandelier	lampadario (m)
fluorescent light	luce fluorescente (f)
hanging light	lampada a sospensione (f)
lamp	lampada (f)
light	luce (f)
light socket	alloggiamento (m)
light switch	interruttore (m)

lighting	illuminazione (f)
reading lamp	lampada da lettura
standard lamp	lampada a stelo
spot light	faretto a parete (m)
wall light	lampada da parete (f)

Gli attrezzi – tools

cable detector	rilevatore cavi (m)
current tester	tester (m) di corrente
insulating tape	nastro isolante (m)
meter	pinza amperometrica (f)
voltage testing screwdriver	cacciavite (m) provacircuiti
wire cutters/strippers	tagliafili/pinza (f) spellafili

08

i lavori di
decorazione
— decorating

Almost the same...

Italian style in decoration and furnishings is very different to ours. Obviously, you will find a huge variety and range of styles in people's houses in Italy, just as you will in the UK, and these ranges largely overlap. (You can't escape IKEA.) But, walk round the popular decoration and furnishing stores in both countries and you will see what we mean. Italian furniture and furnishings tend to be less ornate, wallpaper is very rarely used, internal walls are mostly painted white and floors are mainly tiled or wood-covered.

We are not saying that you should try for an Italian look because it is an Italian house. It's your house, so it should have your look. What we are saying is this. Don't expect to find the same colours and patterns at Bricofer that you would in B & Q, and don't whinge about it.

Check at the comune

* If you are thinking about painting the outside walls or the shutters, look around at your neighbours' houses first. If they all use the same colours, or a very restricted range of colours, the *comune* may have rules on external decorations. Ask at the *comune* before you paint anything. It will only take 10 minutes and it could save you days of repainting.

* Likewise, if you live within sight of a historic building, check at the *comune* before you paint the outside.

Le pitture – paint

Italy is the largest paint producer in Western Europe, which means that the quality of the paint available in shops is very high, although the colour ranges are very different.

If a paint is *ad acqua*, it is water-based – and most is as the Italians rarely use oil-based paint. Other types of paints are *acriliche* (acrylic, of course), *microporose* (for external woodwork) and special paints for *pavimenti* (floors), *soffitti* (ceilings), *metallo* (metal), *scuri* (shutters) and *esterni* (exterior walls).

L'aspetto (the finish) can be *opaco* (matt), *satinato* (satin), *ad effetto rasato* (silk) or *lucido* (gloss).

If you want a non-drip paint, ask for *antigocciolamento*, and for one-coat paint, ask for *monostrato*. (And good luck to you – one coat never does it for us, with either Italian or British paints!)

a effetto rasato	silk
a spruzzo	aerosol
acquaragia (f)	white spirit
acrilica	acrylic
ad acqua	water-based paint
antigocciolamento	non-drip
aspetto (m)	finish, e.g. l'aspetto opaca
campioncino (m) di pittura	test pot
fondo (m)	undercoat
impregnante di fondo (m)	primer
lucida	gloss
microporosa	microporous
monostrato	one-coat
mordente (m) per legno	wood stain
opaca	matt
pittura (f)	paint
pittura per esterni	house paint
satinata	satin finish
smalto (m)	varnish
trementina (f)	turpentine

Gli attrezzi – tools

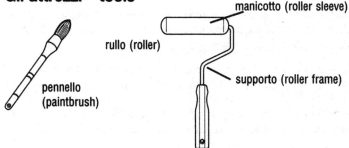

manicotto (roller sleeve)

rullo (roller)

supporto (roller frame)

pennello (paintbrush)

bacinella (f)	paint tray
detergente per pennelli	brush cleaner
manicotto (m)	roller sleeve
manico telescopico (m)	telescopic handle (for roller)
nastro (m) adesivo per mascheratura	masking tape
pennello (m)	brush
rullo (m)	roller
straccio (m)	rag
supporto (m)	roller frame
telone (m)	dust sheet

I rivestimenti per pareti – wall coverings

Wallpaper and wall textiles are not much used in Italy. Wall coverings make rooms warmer, so are really not required in a hot country. Also, the practice of using wallpaper to hold together (minor) cracks on walls and ceilings is not known in Italy.

adesivo (m)	paste
carta da parati (f)	wallpaper
carta di rivestimento	lining paper
carta da parati vinilica	vinyl wallpaper
carta da parati adesiva	ready-pasted wallpaper
cotone (m)	cotton
feltro (m)	flannel/felt
lana (f)	wool
lino (m)	linen
piastrella di sughero (f)	cork tile
rivestimento per pareti (m)	wall covering
seta (f)	silk
tela di canapa (f)	hessian
tessuto (m)	fabric covering
tessuto da parati	wall textile
velluto (m)	velvet

Parati and parete

Parete is a wall, but wall paper is *carta da parati*. This is not a strange misspelling – *parati* is derived from a word meaning 'tapestry'.

Gli attrezzi – tools

pennello per incollare
(pasting brush)

forbici (scissors)

metro a nastro (measuring tape)

filo a piombo (plumb line)

livella a bolla (spirit level)

incollatore per bordi
(seam roller)

corda (f)	string
filo a piombo (m)	plumb line
forbici (f)	scissors
incollatore per bordi (m)	seam roller
livella a bolla (f)	spirit level
metro a nastro (m)	measuring tape
pennello per incollare (m)	pasting brush
pennello per carta da parati	wallpaper brush
scartatrice a vapore (f)	paper stripper
spatola da stucco	filling knife

spugna (f)	sponge
taglierino (m)	Stanley knife
tavolo per incollare (m)	pasting table

La piastrellatura – tiling

Floor tile quality

With tiles playing such a major role in the decoration of Italian houses – not just in bathrooms and kitchens but in all other rooms as well – it's hardly surprising that their quality is determined on the basis of several criteria. These are:

- **PEI scale:** rates tiles for abrasion resistance on a scale of 1 to 5 , with 5 being the most resilient.

- **Mohs scale:** determines the hardness of a tile's surface and is rated from 1 to 10, with 5 denoting a good hardness level.

- **Newton scale:** rates tiles for load resistance on a scale of 20 to 50 (35/38 denotes a good level of strength).

- **Class 1, 2, 3:** this determines stain resistance, where Class 1 is the highest.

- **A, B, C, D scale:** denotes chemical resistance, where A is the highest.

adesivo per piastrelle (m)	tile cement
piastrella (f)	tile
piastrella ceramica	ceramic tile
piastrella per pareti	wall tile
piastrella per pavimenti	floor tile
piastrella di marmo	marble tile
piastrella di sughero	cork tile
piastrella di cotto	terra-cotta tile
piastrella di gres	earthenware tile
piastrella di gres rosso	quarry tile
piastrella di maiolica	majolica tile
piastrellatura delle pareti	wall tiling

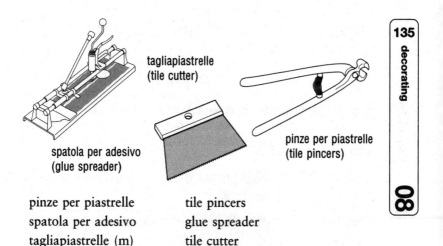

tagliapiastrelle
(tile cutter)

pinze per piastrelle
(tile pincers)

spatola per adesivo
(glue spreader)

pinze per piastrelle   tile pincers
spatola per adesivo   glue spreader
tagliapiastrelle (m)   tile cutter

I rivestimenti per pavimenti – floor coverings

The Italians simply do not use carpets and vinyls as much as we do, so don't expect to find the same choices or the same prices. The traditional Italian house has tiled floors in the kitchen, bathroom, conservatory and similar hard-worn places, and solid parquet or, more frequently, marble and other types of tiles, elsewhere. Learn from the locals. They have been living with their climate all their lives. Bare tiled and wood floors are cooler in the summer and easy to keep clean all year round.

moquette (f)   carpet, just in case you want it
parquet (m)   wood flooring (solid or laminates)
parquet inchiodato   wood floor, fastened by nails
parquet in legno massiccio   solid wood flooring
pavimento (m)   flooring
… laminato (m)   laminate flooring
… laminato con bordi   click-together laminate (literally
maschio e femmina   'with masculine and feminine
                              edges')
… vinilico   vinyl flooring
tappeto (m)   rug

Tende e tende avvolgibili a rullo – curtains and blinds

If you have shutters, you don't need any curtains, except perhaps net ones to give you some privacy when the shutters and windows are open – though that doesn't mean that you can't have them if you want them. They can be a key part of a decorative scheme, and can improve the acoustics of a room.

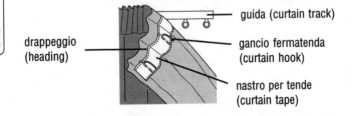

guida (curtain track)

drappeggio
(heading)

gancio fermatenda
(curtain hook)

nastro per tende
(curtain tape)

Inward-opening windows may make it difficult to hang curtains, but they make it almost impossible to fit blinds across the whole aperture. The simple solution is to fit blinds directly to the windows.

Don't forget that in many areas of Italy you will need to install *zanzariere* (mosquito nets) on all windows if you want to sleep at night. The alternatives – mosquito coils and other chemical repellents are toxic and the eco-friendly varieties don't really work.

mantovana (f)	curtain pelmet
gancio fermatenda (m)	curtain hook
nastro per tende (m)	curtain tape
tenda avvolgibile a rullo	blind
veneziana	venetian blind
drappeggio (m)	heading
guida (f)	curtain track
guida metallica	metal curtain track
bacchetta (f)	curtain rod
tulle (m)	netting
tendine di tulle (f)	net curtains

I mobili – furniture

**La sala da pranzo e il soggiorno– the dining room and
living room**

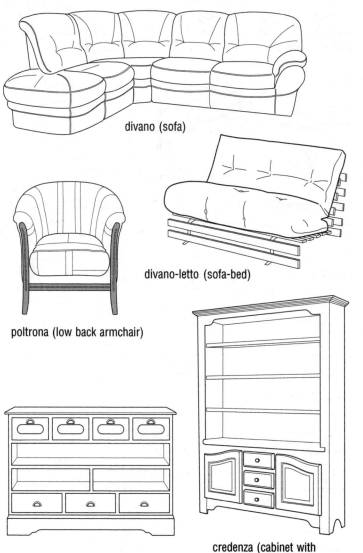

divano (sofa)

divano-letto (sofa-bed)

poltrona (low back armchair)

dispensa (dresser)

credenza (cabinet with
shelves and cupboards)

La camera da letto – the bedroom

cassettiera (chest of drawers)

lampada da letto
(bedside light)

piumone (duvet)

comodino
(bedside cabinet)

letto (bed)

letto a soppalco (raised bed)

cassapanca (chest)

I mobili – furniture

armadietto (m)	small cabinet
argentiera (f)	part-glazed cabinet, for silverware
armadio (m)	wardrobe or large cupboard
canna (f)	cane, rattan
cassapanca (m)	chest
cassettiera (f)	chest of drawers
cassettone (m)	tall set of drawers
comodino (m)	bed side cabinet

credenza (f)	sideboard, dresser, set of shelves and cupboards
cuscino (m)	pillow
dispensa (f)	dining room cupboard/dresser
divano (m)	sofa
divano-letto (m)	sofa-bed
etagere (f)	standing set of shelves
lampada da letto (f)	bedside light
letto (m)	bed
letto a baldacchino (m)	four-poster bed
letto a soppalco (m)	raised bed
libreria (f)	bookcase
materasso (m)	mattress
mobiletto (m)	small cupboard
mobiletto d'entrata	small cupboard, typically placed by entrance door
mobiletto per hi-fi	hi-fi cabinet
panca (f)	bench
panchetta (f)	low bench in bedroom
piumone (m)	duvet
poltrona (f)	easy chair, armchair
sedia (f)	chair
seggio (m)	seat
tavolo (m)	table
tavolino (m)	coffee table
toletta con specchiera (f)	dressing table
vetrina (f)	showcase

English-Italian quick reference

Le pitture – paint

brush	pennello (m)
dust sheet	telone (m)
gloss	lucida

house paint	pittura per esterni (f)
non-drip	antigocciolamento
one-coat	monostrato
paint tray	bacinella
rag	straccio (m)
primer	impregnante di fondo (m)
roller	rullo (m)
undercoat	fondo (m)
turpentine	trementina (f)
varnish	smalto (m)
wood stain	mordente per legno (m)

I rivestimenti per pareti – wall coverings

cork tile	piastrella di sughero (f)
filling knife	spatola da stucco (f)
lining paper	carta di rivestimento (f)
measuring tape	metro a nastro (m)
paper stripper	scartatrice a vapore (f)
pasting brush	pennello per incollare (m)
pasting table	tavolo per incollare (m)
plumb line	filo a piombo (m)
scissors	forbici (f)
seam roller	incollatore per bordi (f)
spirit level	livella a bolla (f)
sponge	spugna (f)
Stanley knife	taglierino (m)
string	corda (f)
textile, for walls	tessuti da parati (m)
vinyl wallpaper	carta da parati vinilica
wallpaper	carta da parati
wallpaper, ready-pasted	carta da parati adesiva
wallpaper paste	adesivo per carta da parati (m)
wallpaper brush	pennello per incollare

La piastrellatura – tiling

ceramic tile	ceramica
cork tile	sughero
earthenware tile	gres
floor tile	piastrella per pavimenti
glue spreader	spatola per adesivo
marble tile	marmo
quarry tile	piastrella in gres rosso
terra-cotta tile	piastrella di cotto
tile	piastrella (f)
tile cutter	tagliapiastrelle (m)
tile cement	adesivo (m) per piastrelle
tile pincers	pinze (f) per piastrelle
wall tile	piastrella (m) per pareti

I rivestimenti per pavimenti – floor coverings

carpet	moquette (f)
laminate flooring	pavimento laminato (m)
nailed wood floor	parquet inchiodato
rug	tappeto (m)
solid wood flooring	parquet in legno massiccio
vinyl flooring	pavimento vinilico
wood flooring	parquet

Tende e tende avvolgibili a rullo – curtains and blinds

blind	tenda avvolgibile a rullo (f)
curtain	tenda
curtain hook	gancio fermatenda (m)
curtain pelmet	mantovana (f)
curtain rod	bacchetta (f)
curtain tape	nastro per tende (m)
curtain track	guida (f)
curtain track, metal	guida metallica
heading (of curtain)	drappeggio

net curtains · tende di tulle (f)

venetian blind · veneziana

I mobili – furniture

armchair · poltrona (f)

bed · letto (m)

bed side cabinet · comodino (m)

bedside light · lampada da letto (f)

bench · panca (f)

bookcase · libreria (f)

chair · sedia (f)

chest · cassapanca (f)

chest of drawers · cassettiera (f)

coffee table · tavolino (m)

cupboard · dispensa (f)

cupboard, small · mobiletto (m)

dressing table · toletta con specchiera (f)

dresser · credenza (f)

duvet · piumone (m)

easy chair · poltrona (f)

hi-fi cabinet · mobiletto per h-fi

low bench for bedroom · panchetta (f)

mattress · materasso (m)

pillow · cuscino (m)

seat · seggio (m)

set of shelves · etagere (f)

sideboard · buffet (m)

sofa · divano (m)

sofa-bed · divano-letto (m)

table · tavolo (m)

wardrobe · armadio (m)

09

il giardino –
the garden

Almost the same...

The lawn is generally the centre of a British garden, but in much of Italy it's too hot and dry to keep a lawn green through the summer without regular watering. If you don't have your own spring or well to draw from, you'll be paying for every drop of that metered water used by the *spruzzatore girevole* (sprinkler) – and that's assuming you're allowed to use it. There are often hosepipe bans during dry spells. Besides, will you be there to water it and cut it? If not, who is going to be there to look after it for you, and at what cost?

For people buying a home in a *complesso residenziale* (housing complex) this won't present a real problem – communal garden areas will be tended by contractors under the terms of your service charge. The only thing you'll need to worry about is looking after your pot plants, which can be hooked up to an *annaffiatoio semiautomático* – a big container of water with spidery hosepipes running off to all your pots, keeping them drip-fed until you come back.

For those of you planning to cultivate a plot with a bit more greenery, ask yourself what you want it to do for you, and what your limitations are. Is it ornamental or do you want to be able to add ice and a slice of your very own lemons to your afternoon *bibita* (drink)? What's the temperature range in your area? How much of the year are you going to spend there, and is there anyone nearby you can persuade to pop over and do the watering now and then for you?

Peer over the fence and see how your neighbours use their gardens. What are they growing? You may be able to do more than you think, even if you're not there to water and weed regularly. Some fruit trees survive remarkably well in poor, dry soil and still produce a lovely crop – the *mandorlo* (almond) or *olivo* (olive) for instance, or perhaps a citrus – an *arancio* (orange) or a *limone* (lemon). How about a *vite* (grape vine)?

For most Brits in Italy, the most important parts of the garden are not the lawn and the veg plot, but the swimming pool and the patio. Lazy afternoons by the pool and summer evenings sipping a nice cold *bibita* and eating olives on the patio with friends. Isn't that why you bought the place?

Check at the comune

- Walls, fences and outbuildings may be subject to planning controls. If you want to build a substantial one, you may need approval.

- A swimming pool will also need planning approval – and may well increase your local property tax.

I muri, i recinti e le siepi – walls, fences and hedges

If you have bought a plot of land, the only thing marking it off from your neighbours may be a line in the sand (literally). While I'm all for being friendly with the people next door, you will probably want something more substantial than that. Regulations vary from region to region and in some parts you will need planning permission to erect walls, gates or any type of fencing other than temporary chain-link fences, walls with no foundations or post fences.

The best way to start – as always – it to look around you. What do the locals have around their properties? Would this suit you? If so, you can almost certainly go ahead without worrying. If you want to build something that is very different, go and talk to the *comune* first.

balaustra in pietra (f)	stone balustrade
bambù (m)	bamboo
cancello (m)	gate
muro (m)	wall (stone)
paletto di recinzione (m)	fence post
pannello a graticcio (m)	latticed fencing panel
pannello di recinzione (m)	fencing panel
recinto (m)	fence
recinto a rete metallica (m)	mesh fencing
siepe (f)	hedge
staccionata (f)	rail fence

La piscina – the swimming pool

For many people, a swimming pool is an essential part of any home in the sun. Installing one is quite simple – just decide how big it should be, where it should go and how much you are willing to pay and get a professional to do the job! It won't be cheap – expect to pay at least €15,000 for a decent-sized pool – and it will need regular maintenance, which will take time and money. But the pool will add value to the house, if you ever come to resell it, and you cannot put a price on the pleasure it will give to you and your guests.

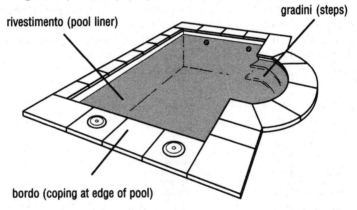

rivestimento (pool liner)

gradini (steps)

bordo (coping at edge of pool)

Some things to consider when planning your pool – discuss these with the pool builder:

• Should you opt for a salt water pool? Salt water discourages algae and needs lower chlorine levels, but can corrode metal pipes and machinery.

♦ What kind of summer and winter covers will the pool need?

Will you be able to manage to haul a plastic cover off by hand or would it be better to fit a roller? If you're feeling really flash, how about a *copertura telescopica* – a glazed roof on runners which slides open or closed as needed!

♦ Where will the pump and filtration unit go? Is there a convenient place in the outbuildings or do you need a pump house?

♦ How big, and what shape? Curved pools can add 10% or more to the cost, but are easier to clean – no corners to stymie robot cleaners.

♦ Do you want a pre-formed pool liner or a custom-made concrete structure? What will you cover it with – pool paint, ceramic tiles or mosaic?

The cost of a pool can vary enormously, so many of these questions are best left until you've answered the first and most important ones: what's your *bilancio* (budget)? Who will use the pool, for what, and how often?

Make sure you or your builders get a *permesso di costruzione* (building permit) for the pool – unless it's a *piscina smontabile* (temporary pool, erected or inflated above ground). If you get your pool builders involved early in the process, they can guide you through the paperwork, or handle it for you.

bilancio (m)	budget
bordo (m)	edge of pool
cloro (m)	chlorine
copertura (f)	cover
depuratore (m)	purification unit
filtro a sabbia (m)	sand filter
gradini (mpl)	steps
prodotto antialghe (m)	anti-algal product
piastrelle (fpl)	tiles
piastrelle a mosaico	mosaic tiling
piscina in cemento (f)	concrete-built pool
piscina smontabile (f)	temporary pool
pittura per piscine (f)	pool-lining paint
pompa (f)	pump

recinto di protezione (m)	safety fence
rivestimento (m)	pool liner
rivestimento sagomato (m)	moulded pool liner
robot pulisci piscine (m)	pool cleaning robot
tavolato (m)	decking
trattamenti chimici (mpl)	chemical treatments

Pool robots come in weird and wonderful shapes, but all work in much the same way. They are powered by the main pump and wander across the bottom and up the sides, dislodging and hoovering up sediment.

I mobili per il giardino – garden furniture

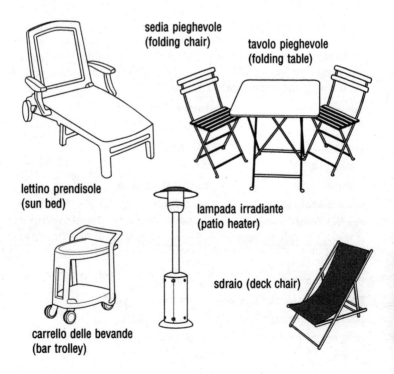

sedia pieghevole
(folding chair)

tavolo pieghevole
(folding table)

lettino prendisole
(sun bed)

lampada irradiante
(patio heater)

sdraio (deck chair)

carrello delle bevande
(bar trolley)

alluminio (m)	aluminium
amaca (f)	hammock
barbecue (m)	barbeque
carrello delle bevande (m)	bar trolley
cuscino (m)	cushion
divano a dondolo (m)	swing seat
ghisa (f)	cast iron
lampada di sicurezza (f)	security light
lampada irradiante (f)	patio heater
lettino prendisole (m)	sun bed
luce da giardino (f)	garden light
materasso (m)	mattress (for sun bed)
ombrellone (m)	sunshade / parasol
sdraio (m)	deck chair
sedia pieghevole (f)	folding chair
tavolo pieghevole (m)	folding table
vasca per la sabbia (m)	sand pit

luce da giardino (garden light) – and remember that
solar powered ones work very well in the Italian climate

Il giardinaggio – gardening

Garden centres are not as common in Italy as they are in the UK
– traditionally, urbanites live in garden-less apartments, while in
the countryside cultivating land is a job, not a hobby. However,
enough people have small gardens or extensive pot plant collec-
tions these days, so you should be able to find somewhere which
stocks plants and seeds, pots, compost, tools and so on.

+ The larger *negozi di fai-da-te* (DIY stores) usually have a gardening section.

+ In rural areas there are agricultural retailers who also handle
  gardening supplies. These can be very good value.

+ If you want trees and shrubs, go to the *serra* (nursery).

Le erbe aromatiche – herbs

aneto (m)	dill
basilico (m)	basil
coriandolo (m)	coriander
erba cipollina (f)	chives
finocchio (m)	fennel
maggiorana (f)	marjoram
menta (f)	mint
prezzemolo (m)	parsley
timo (m)	thyme

Water, water, nowhere...

To help cope with the arid summers in many parts of Italy, there are plenty of ingenious water-efficient devices for watering on the market. Go for *impianti di irrigazione sotterrraneo* (porous underground pipes) or *impianti di irrigazione a goccia* (drip watering systems), and make sure they're *automatizzati* if you're not around much. Many systems come with a *sensore di pioggia* (rain sensor) which cuts off the water supply when it's not needed.

Gli attrezzi – tools

a benzina	with a petrol motor
annaffiatoio (m)	watering can
arieggiatore (m)	scarifier
avvolgitubo (m)	roller for hosepipe
carriola (f)	wheelbarrow
cesoie (fpl)	secateurs, shears
contenitore (m) per acqua piovana	water barrel
decespugliatrice (f)	strimmer
fertilizzante (m)	fertiliser
fontana (f)	fountain

tagliaerba aeroscivolante (hover mower)

decespugliatrice (strimmer)

spruzzatore girevole (oscillating sprinkler)

tagliasiepi (hedge trimmer)

cesoie (shears)

rastrello (lawn rake)

forca (f)	gardening fork
impianto di irrigazione (m)	watering, irrigation
... a gocce (m)	drop-by-drop watering system
... sotterraneo (m)	underground watering pipes
inceneritore (m)	incinerator
motosega (f)	chain saw
paletta da giardinaggio (f)	potting trowel
porta attrezzi (m)	tool shed
prolunga (f)	extension lead
rastrello (m)	rake
scopa da giardino (f)	garden brush
semente (f)	seed
sensore di pioggia (m)	rain sensor
serra (m)	greenhouse
sminuzzatrice (f)	shredder
spruzzatore girevole (m)	sprinkler
stagno (m)	pond
tagliabordi (m)	border trimmer
tagliaerba (m)	mower
tagliaerba aeroscivolante	hover mower
tagliasiepi (m)	hedge trimmer

tappeto erboso (m)	lawn
terreno (f)	soil
trattorino tagliaerba (m)	ride-on mower
tubo per annaffiare (m)	hose
vanga (f)	spade
vaso (m)	pot

English–Italian quick reference

Walls, fences and hedges – i muri, i recinti e le siepi

fence	recinto (m)
fence post	paletto (m)
fence rail	stecca (f)
fencing panel	pannello di recinzione (m)
gate	cancello (m)
hedge	siepe (f)
mesh fencing	recinzione a rete metallica (f)
wall	muro (m)

Swimming pool – la piscina

chlorine	cloro (m)
cover	copertura (f)
decking	tavolato (m)
edge of pool	bordo (m)
mosaic tiling	piastrellatura a mosaico (f)
pool liner, moulded	rivestimento sagomato (m)
pool liner, sheet	rivestimento in teli di PVC (m)
pool paint	pittura per piscine (f)
pump	pompa (f)
safety fence	recinto di protezione (m)
sand filter	filtro a sabbia (m)
steps	gradini (mpl)
tiles	piastrelle (fpl)

Garden furniture – i mobili per il giardino

aluminium	alluminio (m)
bar trolley	carrello per le bevande (m)
cushion	cuscino (m)
deck chair	sdraio (m)
folding chair	sedia pieghevole (f)
folding table	tavolo pieghevole (m)
garden light	lampada da giardino (f)
mattress (for sun bed)	materasso (m)
sand pit	vasca per la sabbia (f)
sun bed	lettino prendisole (m)
security light	lampada di sicurezza (f)
swing seat	divano a dondolo (m)

Cooking herbs – le erbe aromatiche

basil	basilico (m)
chives	erba cipollina (f)
coriander	coriandolo (m)
dill	aneto (m)
fennel	finocchio (m)
marjoram	maggiorana (f)
mint	menta (f)
parsley	prezzemolo (m)
thyme	timo (m)

Gardening – il giardinaggio

almond tree	mandorlo (m)
extension lead	prolunga (m)
fertiliser	fertilizzante (m)
fountain	fontana (f)
garden brush	scopa da giardino (f)
gardening fork	forca (f)
grape vine	vite (f)

greenhouse	serra (f)
hedge trimmer	tagliasiepi (m)
hose	tubo per annaffiare (f)
hover mower	tagliaerba aeroscivolante (m)
incinerator	inceneritore da giardino (m)
lawn	tappeto erboso (m)
lemon tree	limone (m)
mower	tagliaerba (m)
olive tree	olivo (m)
orange tree	arancio (m)
pot	vaso (m)
potting trowel	paletta da giardinaggio (f)
rake	rastrello (m)
ride-on mower	trattorino tagliaerba (m)
roller (for hosepipe)	avvolgitubo (m)
seed	semente (f)
shears	cesoie (fpl)
shredder	sminuzzatrice (f)
soil	terreno (m)
spade	vanga (f)
sprinkler	spruzzatore girevole (m)
strimmer	decespugliatrice (f)
tool shed	porta attrezzi (m)
water barrel	annaffiatoio (m)
wheelbarrow	carriola (f)

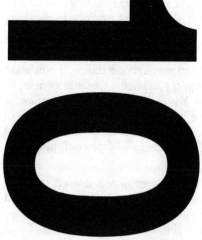

10

un'ora di italiano – an hour of Italian

The CD and the book

This chapter and the CD are built around the same sets of words, and should be used together. The CD gives practice in speaking and listening; the book links the written word to the spoken word.

The aim of this chapter is not to teach you Italian – if you want to learn the language properly, try a *Michel Thomas* course, or one of the titles in the *Teach Yourself* series, such as *Italian* or *Instant Italian*. The aim here is to provide you with a core of words and phrases that will help you to find what you need when you are buying, building, maintaining or equipping your Italian home.

If you already speak Italian to a greater or less degree, we hope that this chapter will give you a firmer grasp of those specialist words that the householder needs. Skip the rest of this section and go straight to *La ricerca – the search* (page 163) and Track 2 on the CD.

Speaking and listening

When you speak Italian to a native, don't try too hard to get a perfect accent. If the Italians think that you can speak their language well, they won't make allowance when they talk to you. And you need them to make allowances! Italian people tend to talk quickly – you need them to slow down so that you can distinguish each word or phrase from the next. Rehearse what you want to say, in your head, let it flow out smoothly, then stand there like an idiot after they reply, without a clue as to what they said.

Speak slowly yourself, and let them hear from your accent that you are a foreigner, and they might speak more slowly and clearly to you. If necessary, ask them to slow down.

Here's your first – and most essential – Italian phrase:

di nuovo e più lentamente   again and more slowly

To which you could add, politely:

per favore   please, literally 'as a favour'

What follows is a brief guide to basic pronunciation. Listen to the CD while you are working through this.

Consonants

The Italians pronounce **every** letter. Italian is a highly phonetic language which means that it is spoken exactly as it's written. Consonants are pronounced as in English, with these exceptions:

c is **k** if followed by *o, a, h* or *u*

la cucina	the kitchen
la chiave	the key

c is **ch** if followed by *e* or *i*

la cerniera	the hinge
la quercia	the oak tree

c is **sh** if preceded by an *s* and followed by *e* or *i*

la piscina	the swimming pool
il saliscendi	the sash window

g is soft (as in 'gerbil') if followed by *e* and *i*

l'agenzia	the (estate) agents
il giardino	the garden

g is hard (as in 'gutter') if followed by *a,* o, *u* or *h*

il gancio	the hook
il righello	the ruler

gn is like the **ny** in the word 'canyon'

il bagno	the bathroom

gl is **ly**

il ripostiglio	the storeroom

Vowels

Vowels are pronounced phonetically as well:

a is **a** as in 'had'

armadio	cupboard

e is **e** as in 'yes'

elettricità	electricity

i   is **i** as in 'fix'

immobile	building

o is **o** as in 'pot'

orologio	clock

u is as **iew** in 'view'

ufficio	office

Gender and endings

Nouns are either masculine or feminine. As a general rule, words that end in *o* or *e* are masculine and words that end in *a* or *ione* are feminine, but that leaves a lot that you just have to know.

A noun's gender affects the words around it. For 'the' you use *il* (or *lo* if it begins with *z*, *gn* or *sc*) if the noun is masculine, and *la* if it is feminine. These apply if a noun begins with a consonant. If it begins with a vowel, the *il* and *la* change to *l'* (e.g. *l'armadio*, *l'elettricità*, *l'immobile*). Likewise 'a' is either *un* (m) or *una* (f).

But if there's more than one of them, it's *i* if the word starts with a consonant (masculine) or *le* (feminine).

For example, *casa* (house) is feminine, and *mulino* (mill) is masculine. That gives us:

the house	*la casa*	the mill	*il mulino*
a house	*una casa*	a mill	*un mulino*
the houses	*le case*	the mills	*i mulini*

If the word starts with a vowel or with *z*, *gn* and *sc* then the masculine article in the plural becomes *gli* instead of 'i'. For example:

the buildings	*gli immobili*
the offices	*gli uffici*
the doormats	*gli zerbini*
the steps	*gli scalini*

Try not to get too hung up on the gender thing. If you say *il casa*, instead of *la casa*, an Italian will know what you mean, though they may find your rendering hilarious.

Adjectives have a different ending if a noun is feminine. Usually, it's just a matter of changing the ending from an *o* or an *e* to an *a*. For example, *bello* means 'beautiful', so 'a beautiful house' – which is feminine – becomes *una bella casa* or *una casa bella*. (The adjective is often placed after the noun.)

The endings of adjectives also change with plural nouns – and usually by just changing the *i* to an *e*.

| the beautiful houses | *le belle case* |
| the small mills | *i piccoli mulini* |

Verbs

Italian verbs 'conjugate'. Their endings, and sometimes the whole word, change depending upon who is doing the thing and when they are doing it. Verbs also conjugate in English, but not as much. The infinitive of all Italian verbs end in *are*, *ere* or *ire* and the regular ones follow patterns. Unfortunately an awful lot of Italian verbs are irregular and have to be learnt by heart.

Parlare (to talk) is a regular verb. Here's how it conjugates:

io parlo	I talk
tu parli	you talk
lei parla	you talk (polite form, see boxed item)
egli/ella parla	he/she talks
noi parliamo	we talk
voi parlate	you talk
essi/esse parlano	they (masculine/feminine) talk

All other regular verbs that end in *are* conjugate in the same way, so to say these, chop off the *are* and add the appropriate ending from the list shown above. For example, with *domandare* (to ask), you would say *io domando* (I ask), *tu domandi*, *egli domanda*, etc. (Or simply, *domando*, *domandi*, *domanda*, etc, as the Italians often miss out the personal pronoun.)

All regular verbs that end in *ere* or *ire*, conjugate as follows:

vedere (to see)

io vedo	I see
tu vedi	you see
lei/egli/ella vede	you/he/she sees
noi vediamo	we see
voi vedete	you see
essi/esse vedono	they (m/f) see

Lei and tu – which you?

The Italians have two words for 'you'. *Lei* is used when speaking to someone to show respect. *Tu* should only be used when speaking to a child or a friend. It's rude to *dare del tu* to someone (use *tu* instead of *lei*) if you are not familiar with them.

sentire (to hear)

io sento	I hear
tu senti	you hear
lei/egli/ella sente	you/he/she hears
noi sentiamo	we hear
voi sentite	you hear
essi/esse sentono	they (m/f) hear

All other regular verbs that end in *ere* or *ire* conjugate in the same way, so to say these, just replace the ending with one to match the personal pronoun. For example, with *vivere* (to live) you would say *vivo, vivi, vive, viviamo*, etc., whereas *dormire* (to sleep) conjugates *dormo, dormi, dorme, dormiamo*, etc.

Many verbs are highly irregular, and you should at least be aware of these two.

essere – to be

io sono	I am
tu sei	you are
lei/egli/ella è	you/he/she is
noi siamo	we are
voi siete	you are
essi/esse sono	they (m/f) are

avere – to have

io ho	I have
tu hai	you have
lei/egli/ella ha	you/he/she has
noi abbiamo	we have
voi avete	voi avete
essi/esse hanno	they (m/f) have

We've only looked at the present tense. There are also several ways of talking about past and future events, all of which affect the shape and sound of the verb. And there are lots of irregularities to the way they conjugate, so take our advice: live in the present, never write anything down, and just change the verbs ending to suit the personal pronoun. If nothing else, you will amuse the locals, and when they've stopped laughing, they'll be pleased to help you.

non – not

To say 'not' you need just one word, *non*, which goes before the verb. Bear in mind that the pronoun which in English precedes the verb is normally omitted in Italian. For example:

I am not...   *non sono...*

Here's a 'not' phrase you may find very useful.

I do not understand   *non capisco*

To say 'not' without a verb, use the same word order:

not today   *non oggi*

Greetings

hello	salve
good evening	buona sera
goodbye	arrivederci
have a good day	buona giornata
thank you	grazie
thank you very much	molte grazie
don't mention it	di niente
pardon me	mi scusi
how do you do?	come va?
fine, thanks	va bene, grazie
I am called...	mi chiamo...

Asking questions

In Italian the word order is the same for statements and questions – it's the tone of your voice when speaking, or the written '?' that makes it a question. So, 'you speak English' is *parla inglese*, and 'do you speak English?' is translated *parla inglese?*

chi (who), *dove* (where), *quale* (what), *quando* (when) and *perché* (why) questions use the same order as in English.

where is the town hall?	dov'è il comune?
it's to the right	è a destra
it's to the left	è a sinistra

it's straight on	sempre dritto
it's over there	è là
it's here	è qui
it's how much?	quant'è?
why?	perché?
this house is cheap, why?	questa casa è a buon mercato, perché?
why is this house so dear?	perchè è così cara questa casa?
how old is this house?	quanti anni ha questa casa?
what time is it?	che ore sono?
it is 7 o'clock	sono le sette in punto
half past eight	sono le otto e mezza
quarter to ten	sono le dieci meno un quarto
at 15.00	alle quindici

(They normally use the 24-hour clock.)

it's lunch time	è l'ora di pranzo
when?, at what time?	a che ora?
on what day?	che giorno?
what date?	in che data?
can we set a date?	possiamo fissare una data?

I numeri – numbers

0	zero	13	tredici	31	trentuno
1	uno	14	quattordici	32	trentadue
2	due	15	quindici	40	quaranta
3	tre	16	sedici	50	cinquanta
4	quattro	17	diciassette	60	sessanta
5	cinque	18	diciotto	70	settanta
6	sei	19	diciannove	80	ottanta
7	sette	20	venti	90	novanta
8	otto	21	ventuno	100	cento
9	nove	22	ventidue	200	duecento
10	dieci	23	ventitrè	1000	mille
11	undici	etc.		2,000	duemila
12	dodici	30	trenta	1,000,000	un milione

Le date – dates

Sunday	domenica	January	gennaio
Monday	lunedì	February	febbraio
Tuesday	martedì	March	marzo
Wednesday	mercoledì	April	aprile
Thursday	giovedì	May	maggio
Friday	venerdì	June	giugno
Saturday	sabato	July	luglio
		August	agosto
tomorrow	domani	September	settembre
today	oggi	October	ottobre
yesterday	ieri	November	novembre
		December	dicembre

La ricerca – the search (Track 2)

Let's start with some words and phrases to help you find that house.

I am looking for...	cerco...
we are looking for...	cerchiamo...
I want to buy...	voglio comprare...
we want to buy...	vogliamo comprare...
...a flat..	...un appartamento...
...a little house...	...una casetta...
...a large house...	...una grande casa...
...in the country...	...di campagna...
...in the town...	...di città...
...to restore...	...da rinnovare
...in good condition	...in buone condizioni
is this house for sale?	questa casa è in vendita?

Defining the house

Three key ways to define a house are its size – measured in square metres of floor space – the number of rooms and its price. You'll need to brush up your numbers for all of these. But if you want to make sure that you've understood the numbers correctly, ask the agents to write them down. Figures don't need translation!

about	circa
more than	più di
less than	meno di
50 m² (cottage size)	cinquanta metri quadri
100 m² (average UK semi)	cento metri quadri
200 m² (large detached)	due cento metri quadri
two bedrooms	due camere da letto
five rooms	cinque camere
€60,000	sessantamila euro
€120,000	cento ventimila euro
€1,000,000	un milione di euro

The features

What features are essential, desirable or to be avoided?

there must be...	deve avere...
is there...	ha/c'è...
...a kitchen	...la cucina
...a bathroom	...il bagno
...a swimming pool	...la piscina
...a garden	...il giardino
...a convertible attic	...la soffitta trasformabile in mansarda
...a cellar	...la cantina
...a beautiful view	...una bella vista
is there...	bisogna (if followed by a verb)...
...work to be done	...fare dei lavori?
is it on the mains drains?	è collegata alla rete fognaria?
is the roof in a good state?	è in buone condizioni il tetto?

Your decision

And what do you think of the property? Do you want to keep looking or is it time to start negotiating the price?

no, thank you	no, grazie
it's too dear	è troppo cara
it's too big/small	è troppo grande/piccola
there is too much to do	c'è troppo lavoro da fare
perhaps	forse
I have other houses to see	ho altre case da vedere
do you have other houses?	avete altre case?
I like this house...	la casa mi piace...
we like this house...	la casa ci piace...
...but not the price	...ma il prezzo no
can we negotiate?	possiamo trattare?
here is my offer	questa è la mia offerta
it's perfect!	è perfetta!
agreed	d'accordo

La vendita – the sale (Track 3)

There is not enough in this book to enable you to handle safely the legal and financial aspects of house purchase. You must have a good grasp of Italian – and of Italian law – or the services of a translator and/or English-speaking lawyer.

Before you commit yourself to the purchase, you may want to check the price, or the cost – and feasibility – of essential works.

could you recommend...	potrebbe consigliarmi...
...a valuer	...un consulente immobiliare
...a master of the works	...un capomastro
...a notary	...un notaio
I need/we need...	ho/abbiamo bisogno di...
...a valuation...	...una valutazione...
...an estimate...	...un preventivo...
...for this house	...per questa casa

(There is more on estimates in the next section, *I lavori* – building work, Track 4.)

You might want to find out the level of the local taxes and/or the service charges in an apartment block, and you should also check who's paying the agent's fees.

where is the town hall?	dov'è il comune?
where is the tax office?	dov'è l'ufficio delle imposte?
how much are...?	quanto sono...?
...the taxes...	...le imposte...
...for this address	...per questo indirizzo
...the service charges of	...le tariffe pubbliche
...the apartment block	...della palazzina
who pays the agency fees?	chi paga la commissione d'agenzia?
the seller pays	la paga il venditore

With your queries answered, you should be ready to commit, though there may be conditions in some cases.

we are ready to buy	siamo disposti a comprare
I want to buy this house...	voglio comprare questa casa...
...at the price of...€ 000	...al prezzo di ...mille euro
...under these conditions	...a queste condizioni
there must be a satisfactory zoning certificate	è necessario un certificato urbanistico in regola
I must get a mortgage	devo ottenere il mutuo
I would like to see the health expert's certificates	vorrei vedere i certificati sanitari
I cannot give you the deposit today	non posso darle la caparra oggi
I will transfer the money from the UK	farò un bonifico bancario dal Regno Unito
when does the cooling-off period start?	quando inizia il periodo di riflessione?

If you want to clarify any points of the sale agreement, or set up a Italian will, you will need to visit the notaio.

where is the notary's office?	dov'è l'ufficio notarile?

do you speak English?	parla inglese?
I would like to make a will	vorrei fare testamento
we want joint ownership of the house	vogliamo acquistare la casa in comproprietà

If they are present, get the water, gas, electricity and telephone accounts transferred to your name at the time of the sale. Ask the *agenzia immobiliare*.

which services are present?	quali servizi ci sono?
can you transfer the accounts to me/to us?	potete trasferire la contabilità a mio /a nostro nome?
which are the rubbish collection days?	quali sono i giorni di raccolta dei rifiuti?
where is the waste collection site?	dov'è il centro di raccolta dei rifiuti?

where is the recycling centre? dov'è il centro di riciclaggio?

And don't forget the *per favore* when you ask a question, or the *grazie* when you get a reply.

I lavori – building work (Track 4)

As long as you hold your meetings on site, armed with a *schizzo* (sketch) or *piano di costruzione* (plan), you can get a long way with a limited vocabulary and lots of hand waving. First find your workforce. Ask at the *agenzia immobiliare* or the *comune*.

can you recommend...	potrebbe consigliarmi...
...an architect	...un architetto
...a project manager	...un capomastro
...a builder	...un muratore
...a (roof) carpenter	...un falegname
...a roofer	...un copritetto
...a joiner	...un carpentiere
...a plumber	...un idraulico
...an electrician	...un elettricista
...a plasterer	...un intonacatore
...a stonemason	...un tagliapietre

Then specify the job on site. Notice that the word for 'new' is *nuovo* if the noun is masculine, or *nuova* if it is feminine.

here are my sketch and plan	ecco lo schizzo e il piano di costruzione
I want...	voglio...
...to knock down the walls	...abbattere i muri
...to knock down these outbuildings	...abbattere queste dependance
...to convert the attic	...trasformare la soffitta in mansarda
...to make two rooms	...creare due camere
the house needs...	la casa ha bisogno di...
...a new roof	...un tetto nuovo
...a new floor	...un pavimento nuovo
I want to build...	voglio costruire...
...a new bathroom	...un nuovo bagno
...a new kitchen	...una nuova cucina
...an extra bedroom	...un'altra camera da letto
...a garage	...un garage
...a swimming pool	...una piscina
this big (with gestures!)	grande così
this high	alta così
can you give me an estimate for this work?	potrebbe farmi un preventivo per i lavori?
when can you do the work?	quando potrebbe realizzare i lavori?

Do you need planning permission or approval of the work?

could you give me...	potrebbe darmi...
...the address of the consultant architect	...l'indirizzo dell'architetto consulente
...a form for...	...un modulo...
...planning permission	...di richiesta del permesso di costruzione
...permission to demolish	...di richiesta del permesso di demolizione
...notice of works	...di denuncia inizio attività

La struttura – the structure

Talking to il muratore – the builder (Track 5)

can you build...	potrebbe costruire...
...a brick wall	...un muro di mattoni
...a partition wall	...una parete divisoria
...a stone chimney	...un camino in pietra
...a reinforced concrete floor	...un pavimento in cemento armato
...a lining for this wall	...un rivestimento per questo muro
can you...	potrebbe...
...renovate the roughcast	...rinnovare il rinzaffo
...repoint the walls	...riempire di calce le commessure dei muri
...do half-timbered walls	...fare i muri in legno e muratura
...work on exposed beams	...fare le travi a vista
there is rising damp	c'è umidità risalente
the house needs a damp course	la casa ha bisogno di una barriera impermeabile

Finding tools and materials at the negozio di Fai-da-Te – the DIY store (Track 6)

where can I find...	dove posso trovare...
...builder's tools	...gli attrezzi da muratore
...a bucket	...un secchio
...a chisel	...uno scalpello
...a filling knife	...una spatola da stucco
...a shavehook	...un raschietto
...a shovel	...una pala
...a spade	...una vanga
...a spirit level	...una livella a bolla
...a trowel	...una cazzuola

...breeze blocks	...i blocchi di cemento cellulare
...bricks	...i mattoni
...cement	...il calcestruzzo
...insulation panels	...i pannelli isolanti
...a lintel	...un'architrave
...plasterboard	...i pannelli di gesso
...plaster blocks	...i blocchi di gesso
...sand	...la sabbia
...stones	...le pietre
...wall ties	...i ferri di collegamento
...wood preservative	...i conservanti per legno
...treatment for mould	...i trattamenti antimuffa
where can I hire a concrete mixer?	dove posso noleggiare una betoniera?

Talking to il falegname – roof carpenter – and il copritetto – the roofer (Track 7)

I would like...	vorrei...
...to convert the attic	...trasformare la soffitta in mansarda
...create a terrace roof	...costruire un tetto a terrazza
can you build...	potrebbe costruire...
...a dormer window	...un'abbaino
...a lathe and plaster ceiling	...un soffitto a listelli e gesso
can you install...	potrebbe installare...
...a skylight	...un lucernaio
...lining felt	...del feltro isolante
...insulation	...l'isolamento
can you renovate...	potrebbe rinnovare...
...these rafters	...questi puntoni
...the joists	...i travicelli
...the roof trusses	...le capriate
...the hip roof	...il tetto a padiglione
...the roof timbers	...le travi del tetto

...the lathing	...i listelli
...the ridge beam	...la trave di colmo
...the valley gutter	...il canale di gronda/la conversa
...the flashing	...la scossallina
...the slate clips	...i naselli di fermo
oak or pine?	di quercia o di pino?
a roof of...	un tetto di...
...flat tiles	...tegole piatte
...curved tiles	...tegole curve
...roofing panels	...pannelli di copertura
...slates	...ardesia

Le opere in legno – woodwork

Talking to il carpentiere – the joiner (Track 8)

here, we would like...	qui, vorremmo...
...a built-in cupboard	...un armadio a muro
...a door with its frame	...una porta con telaio
...panelling	...la pannellatura
...three shelves	...tre mensole
...wood flooring	...il pavimento in legno
...a letter box	...una cassetta per le lettere
can you make...	può costruire...
...a French window	...una porta-finestra
...a skylight	...un lucernaio
...new shutters	...nuovi scuri
...a roller shutter	...una serranda avvolgibile
...a slatted shutter	...una persiana
...a spiral staircase	...una scala a chiocciola
...a new handrail	...una nuova ringhiera
...a fitted wardrobe	...un armadio a muro
...a set of shelves	...delle mensole

Finding materials at the negozio di Fai-da-Te (Track 9)

where can I find...	dove posso trovare...
...chipboard	...i pannelli truciolati
...hardboard	...i pannelli di fibre compresse
...hardwood	...il legno duro
...melamine panels	...i pannelli rivestiti in melamina
...veneer	...i piallicci decorativi
...plywood	...il compensato
...tongue and grooved	...i pannelli con bordi maschio e femmina
...veneered panels	...i pannelli impiallacciati
...wood panels	...i pannelli di legno
...hardware for doors	...i serramenti per porte
...bolts	...i chiavistelli
...cylinder locks	...le serrature a cilindro
...door handles	...le maniglie per porte
...hinges	...le cerniere
...split hinges	...le cerniere estraibili
...strap hinges	...le cerniere a bandella
...mortice locks	...le serrature da infilare
...shutter catches	...i fermascuri
...latches	...i catenacci
...shutter fastenings	...le spagnolette

Finding tools at the negozio di Fai-da-Te (Track 10)

where are the wood tools?	dove sono gli attrezzi per legno?
do you have...	avete...
...chisels	...degli scalpelli
...cutters (Stanley knives)	...dei taglierini
...drill bits	...delle punte da trapano
...electric drills	...dei trapani elettrici
...electric jig saws	...delle seghe da traforo
...electric screwdrivers	...dei cacciavite elettrici
...hammers	...dei martelli

...nails	...dei chiodi
...pincers	...delle tenaglie
...sandpaper	...della carta vetrata
...saws	...delle seghe
...screws	...delle viti
...screwdrivers	...dei cacciaviti
...staple guns	...delle pistole graffettatrici
...tape measures	...dei metri a nastro
...wood glue	...della colla per legno

L'impianto idraulico – plumbing

Talking to l'idraulico – the plumber (Track 11)

can you install...	può montare...
...galvanised gutters	...delle grondaie zincate
...some copper pipes	...dei tubi di rame
...a waste water system	...un impianto di scarico delle acque
...a new joint	...un giunto nuovo
...bathroom fittings	...le attrezzature sanitarie
...a WC	...un WC
...a septic tank	...una fossa biologica
...a soakaway	...un pozzo perdente
...a soil pipe	...un tubo di caduta
where is...	dov'è...
...the stopcock	...il rubinetto di arresto
...the drain cock	...il rubinetto di scarico
...the regulator	...il regolatore
...the water meter	...il contatore dell'acqua
do you know someone who empties septic tanks?	conosce un addetto allo svuotamento delle fosse biologiche?

Shopping for bathroom and kitchen equipment (Track 12)

where can I find...	dove posso trovare...
...basins	...i lavabi
...bathtubs	...le vasche
...medicine cabinets	...gli armadietti dei medicinali
...mirrors	...gli specchi
...mixer taps	...i miscelatori
...a plug	...un tappo
...a rubbish bin	...un cestino per l'immondizia
...showers	...le docce
...taps	...i rubinetti
...towel rails	...i porta-asciugamani
...a washer	...una rondella
...kitchen equipment	...le attrezzature di cucina
...a cooker hood	...una cappa di cucina
...a dishwasher	...una lavastoviglie
...hobs	...i piani di cottura
...kitchen sinks	...i lavelli
...ovens	...i forni
...washing machines	...le lavatrici
...work surfaces	...i piani di lavoro
I would like a sink with two bowls and one drainer	vorrei un lavello a due vasche con scolapiatti

Finding tools at the negozio di Fai-da-Te (Track 13)

I am looking for...	cerco...
...a spanner	...una chiave per dadi
...an adjustable spanner	...una chiave inglese
...cutters (for PVC pipes)	...i tagliatubi
...a hacksaw	...un seghetto
...a mole grip	...una pinza a morsa
...a soldering lamp	...un cannello per saldare

Il riscaldamento e l'elettricità – heating and electricity

Talking to l'impiantista termico – the heating engineer – and l'elettricista – the electrician (Track 14)

can you install...	può installare...
...a fireplace	...un caminetto
...a boiler	...una caldaia
...some radiators	...dei radiatori
...a stove	...una stufa
...central heating	...il riscaldamento centrale
oil-fired	a gasolio
gas-fired	a gas
where can I buy...	dove posso comprare...
...coal	...il carbone
...logs	...dei tronchi di legno
...wood	...la legna
can you recommend	può consigliarmi
a chimney sweep?	uno spazzacamino?
can you rewire the house?	può rifare l'impianto elettrico?
where is/are...	dov'è/dove sono...
...the mains switch	...l'interruttore di rete
...the meter	...il contatore
...the circuit breakers	...gli interruttori di circuito
can you fit...	può montare...
...a socket	...una presa
...a fuse box	...una scatola dei fusibili
...a light switch	...un interruttore
...a plug	...una spina

Shopping for le apparecchiature elettriche – electrical appliances (Track 15)

where can I find...	dove posso trovare...
...convector heaters	...i termoconvettori /convettori di calore

...electric fires	...i caminetti elettrici
...cookers	...le cucine
...DVD players	...i lettori DVD
...food processors	...i robot da cucina/ multifunzioni
...freezers	...i congelatori
...fridges	...i refrigeratori
...kettles	...i bollitori
...irons	...i ferri da stiro
...telephones	...i telefoni
...TVs	...i televisori
...flat screen TVs	...i televisori a schermo piatto
...vacuum cleaners	...le aspirapolveri
...light fittings	...le apparecchiature di illuminazione
...a ceiling light	...una plafoniera
...a bedside light	...una lampada da letto
...a hanging light	...una lampada a sospensione
...a lamp	...una lampada
...a wall light	...una lampada da parete

I lavori di decorazione – decorating

Finding materials at the negozio di Fai-da-Te (Track 16)

where can I find...	dove posso trovare...
...paint	...le pitture
...gloss paint	...la pittura lucida
...masonry paint	...la pittura per esterni
...non-drip paint	...la pittura antigocciolamento
...primer	...la pittura/l'impregnante di fondo
...varnish	...lo smalto
...wood stain	...il mordente per legno

is this one-coat?	questa è pittura monostrato?
do you sell...	vendete...
...wall coverings	...i rivestimenti per pareti
...textiles, for walls	...i tessuti da parati
...wallpaper	...la carta da parati
...cork tiles	...le piastrelle di sughero
...lining paper	...la carta di rivestimento
...tiles	...le piastrelle
...floor tiles	...le piastrelle per pavimenti
...terra-cotta tiles	...le piastrelle di cotto

Finding tools at the negozio di Fai-da-Te (Track 17)

where can I find...	dove posso trovare ...
...a measuring tape	...un metro a nastro
...a paper stripper	...una scartatrice a vapore
...a pasting brush	...un pennello per incollare
...scissors	...le forbici
...a spirit level	...una livella a bolla
...a sponge	...una spugna
...string	...della corda
...wallpaper paste	...l'adesivo per carta da parati
...a wallpaper brush	...un pennello per carta da parati
...brushes	...i pennelli
...paint trays	...le bacinelle
...rollers	...i rulli
where can I find...	dove posso trovare...
...a tile cutter	...un tagliapiastrelle
...a tile cutting machine	...una macchina tagliapiastrelle
...wall tiles	...le piastrelle per pareti

Finding floor coverings, curtains and furniture (Track 18)

| do you sell... | vendete... |
| ...carpets | ...le moquette |

…laminate flooring	…i pavimenti laminati
…rugs	…i tappeti
…vinyl flooring	…i pavimenti vinilici
…wood flooring	…i pavimenti in legno/i parquet
…blinds	…le tende avvolgibili a rullo
…curtains	…le tende
…curtain tracks	…le guide per tende
…net curtains	…le tendine di pizzo
we are looking for…	cerchiamo…
…an armchair	…una poltrona
…some chairs	…delle sedie
…a table	…un tavolo
…a bookcase	…una libreria
…some cupboards	…una credenza/un armadietto
…a sofa-bed	…un divano-letto
…a bed	…un letto
…a chest of drawers	…una cassettiera/un cassettone
…a wardrobe	…un armadio
…duvets	…dei piumoni
…a mattress	…un materasso
…some pillows	…dei cuscini

Il giardino – the garden

Talking to i muratori – the builders (Track 19)

can you build…	potete costruire…
…a fence of panels	…un recinto/una recinzione a pannelli
…a gate	…un cancello
…a wall	…un muro
…a swimming pool…	…una piscina…
…with a moulded liner	…con rivestimento sagomato
…with a sheet liner	…con rivestimento in teli di PVC

the pool needs...	la piscina ha bisogno di...
...coping (for edge of pool)	...pietre di copertura
...a cover	...una copertura
...a pump	...una pompa
...a safety fence	...una recinzione di sicurezza
...a sand filter	...un filtro a sabbia
...some steps	...dei gradini

Shopping for il giardino – the garden (Track 20)

where can I find...	dove posso trovare...
...covers for furniture	...le fodere per mobili da giardino
...deck chairs	...gli sdrai
...floodlights	...i proiettori
...folding chairs	...le sedie pieghevoli
...garden lights	...le luci da giardino
...a patio heater	...una lampada irradiante
...a sand pit	...una vasca per la sabbia
...a sun bed	...un lettino prendisole
...a security light	...una luce/lampada di sicurezza
...an extension lead	...una prolunga
...a garden brush	...una scopa da giardino
...a hedge trimmer	...un tagliasiepi
...a hose	...un tubo per annaffiare
...an incinerator	...un inceneritore da giardino
...mowers	...i tagliaerba
...potting trowels	...le palette da giardinaggio
...a rake	...un rastrello
...a ride-on mower	...un trattorino tagliaerba
...a roller for a hosepipe	...un avvolgitubo
...seeds	...le sementi/i semi
...shears	...le cesoie
...a sprinkler	...uno spruzzatore girevole
...a water barrel	...un contenitore per acqua piovana

Appendix

investimento – investment

Buying for investment

If you are thinking of buying a property in Italy *purely* as an investment, think again. That's not to say don't invest there, just that there are other places that will give you faster capital growth and/or a better regular return. If you are thinking of buying in Italy because you love it and want to spend time there in a place of your own – and also make some money out of your investment, then that's a different story.

House prices in Italy have been rising overall at between 5% and 8% over the last 10 years, and this growth has been largely the result of lower interest rates and increased domestic demand. Brits and other North Europeans are buying there, but not at the same levels as in Spain, France and Portugal. As a result, the UK property price boom of 2000 to 2005 which fuelled huge price increases in the more popular retirement/second homes area did not have much impact in Italy. Having said that, in Italy as in the UK, house prices have risen ahead of inflation, and property has proved to offer a better return than most other forms of investment – and it is reasonable to expect that to continue.

Of course, you can lose money if you are not careful. There are two main dangers: paying too much in the first place, and having to sell in a hurry. Even if you get the price right when buying, you need a sale price of 25% or so higher to show any real profit, once the fees and taxes and other costs are taken into account. On current trends, this could take 5 years or more.

What's that? You can't wait that long? Well, there is a possible alternative.

Buying and selling off-plan

In general terms, buying off-plan is the only way to get a short-term return on property – and that is in no way guaranteed. The properties are usually apartments in a tourist complex, typically in a ski resort, or close to a beach and/or a golf course. The ultimate owners will buy them for their own holiday use and for the rental income which they should generate – but that is not the aim for off-plan buyers.

The theory is this: you agree to buy the apartment when it only exists on the plan, and you pay a deposit of perhaps 10%. You

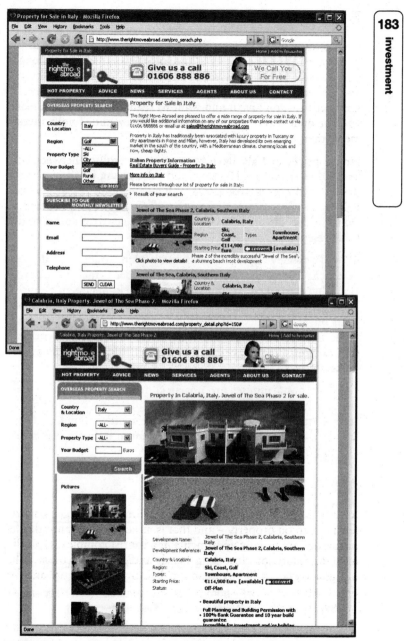

The Right Move Abroad is one of the UK specialists in off-plan investments in Italy.

get a discount for buying early – and the earlier you buy, the bigger the discount. The developer needs those initial sales to raise loans for the construction and to stimulate interest in the project; and you are taking a little more risk than if you bought an actual concrete (as it were) apartment. You will be required to come up with further payments at different stages in the building process – perhaps totalling half the purchase price. You won't need to find the rest of the cash until completion – and you may be able to sell even before that.

If you get it right, the development will be so popular that people will be queuing up to buy it off you, giving you a nice quick profit. If you get it wrong, and pick a development that does not sell out, so prices never rise, or pick a developer who fails to manage the job properly – you may be left with an expensive white elephant.

To make money buying and selling off-plan, you need to do your research. You must check the the developer's track record, find out what happened to similar earlier developments in the area, look carefully at the tourist rental potential, talk to other off-plan buyers and take professional advice. As a fall-back position, you should also think about how long-term ownership would work for you, in case you cannot find a buyer at a good price.

Off-plan opportunities are not as common in Italy as they are in, say, Spain – the tourist market is different – so you have to look a little harder to find them. To see what's around, and read up more on off-plan property investment in Italy, try these sites:

* www.therightmoveabroad.com
* www.propertyshowrooms.com
* www.propertyinvestment.co.uk

Keep an eye on it

If you are thinking about buying, or have bought, an apartment in a development, you may be able to talk to other buyers, and to see photos of the construction as it happens though the EyeonWorld website. Find it at:

http://www.eyeonworld.com

Restoration

There are more opportunities for profit in restoring ruins – though these are very much long-term and energy-intensive projects. The Italian countryside and its villages have lots of empty houses, cottages, *trulli* and other more exotic structures in need of someone to give them a new lease of life. It is possible to pick up a run-down house for £20,000, spend £30,000 on modernising it and sell it for £100,000. Possible, but you need to know what you are doing. In some cases these properties really are ruins, where 'pull down and rebuild' is the only sensible option. Some just need bringing into the 21st century, but even that is not as simple as it might sound. There are three major problems:

- **The paperwork** – Italy is a very bureaucratic state, and building work is very tightly controlled, especially in historic sites and areas of natural beauty. And getting permissions may not just be a matter of filling out the forms correctly – all too often you need to know the right people and to grease the right palms. (Transparency International, an organisation that monitors bribery and corruption in government and the commercial world, rates Italy as 45th out of 163 countries in the corruption league – the worst, by far of Western Europe. Go to **www.transparency.org** for more.)

- **The builders** – in any country, it's difficult to find builders who can do the job to your specifications, to schedule and at the agreed price, and as you get closer to the Mediterranean, it seems to get harder. Get at least three quotes, and look at other work that the builders have done. Talk to people – your estate agent, lawyer, neighbours – and ask for their recommendations. Look for builders at work in the area and watch how they go about the job. It all takes time, but it can save you endless time, worry and money in the long run.

- **The costs** – they can run away if you do not keep them tightly under control. Problems will inevitably arise – you start by stripping off old wallpaper and finish up ripping down the whole wall. The builders will have their own ideas which will increase the cost. And there's always the temptation to add to your original plans – you don't need to say 'well, it's only a couple of thousand extra' many times to go way over budget.

And there are two golden rules:

* Use qualified tradesmen and get – and keep – the invoices. These are your best guarantees against poor work, and they are guarantees that you can hand on to your buyers when you come to sell.

* Restore the house in the local style, using local materials. You want it to stand out as an example of what can be done well, not stick out like a sore thumb. And your potential buyers are probably people who are looking for a traditional Italian house – but in pristine condition. Employ an experienced local architect and follow his advice.

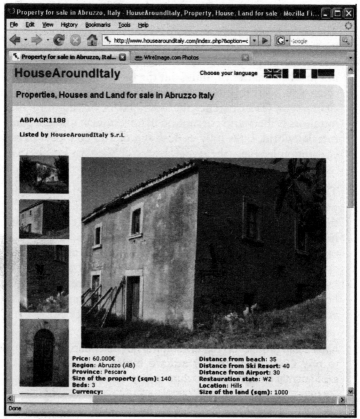

The thing about restoring ruins is that, if you don't mind roughing it at the start, and getting your hands dirty, you can get a lot more for your money. By the way, I don't think those beams are just propped against the wall out of the way.

So, it doesn't have glass in the windows and it needs completely gutting inside, but it's only €40,000 and you've got the beach, skiing and the airport all within 50km. There is lots of choice of restoration projects at HouseAroundItaly.

How much will it cost?

A full scale ground-up restoration will not be cheap – expect to pay £800 or more per square metre, but costs fall significantly if the main structure is in good condition. If you are restoring for sale, keep it simple and avoid extravagances – people will not pay enough extra for gold-plated taps and hand-carved Etruscan walnut newel posts to justify the expense of fitting them.

And when you have restored your ruin, you can put it back on the market at rather more than it will have cost you (as long as you don't count the cost of your energy, worry, arguments, etc.)

Try these sites for restoration projects (and more):

www.housearounditaly.com

www.picenehomes.com

www.tuscanyrealestate.co.uk

Holiday rentals

If you bought your Italian house as a holiday home, two things should follow from this: (1) it's in a nice place to have a holiday, and (2) it will be empty for much of the year. Why not rent it out? Potential rental income varies hugely, of course, depending upon the size, position and features of the house, and on the time of year, and in the quality of the marketing that brings in the visitors. A family-sized villa with a private swimming pool on the coast of Tuscany could rent out at £2500 or more per week in the high season; 3-bedroom apartments in the Marche on the Adriatic coast are currently asking £800 or so a week. It will not be every week, but you should get a higher take-up here

Research your market! Check the bookings of similar properties to get an idea of potential income. At the start of July, this 6-person villa by the Tuscan coast was booked for most of the summer, and would have earned around £35,000 – before costs – in total that year. Other villas in the area showed the same level of activity.

than in France and Spain where the tourist rental market is over-supplied. You should be able to achieve an occupancy rate of 15-20% (8–10 weeks a year), and at least half of that in the high season. That might bring in £15,000 or so for your villa in Tuscany, or possibly £6000 for an apartment.

You will need to find someone local to act as keyholder, cleaner, gardener, poolboy, etc., but those wages are probably about the main extra costs – your house insurance may be higher, and there will be more wear and tear on the contents.

If you want a better idea of the rental income and the occupancy rate that your house might achieve, go to the holiday rental websites, look for similar properties and check their charges and availability. (This is best done in early summer when the bookings should be largely in place.) Try these sites:

http://www.tuscanynow.com

http://homeinitaly.com

http://www.ownersdirect.co.uk/Italy.htm

Taxes

Capital gains

The good news is that capital gains tax was scrapped in Italy in 1993. The bad news is that it was replaced by an annual tax on property, the *Imposta Comunale sugli Immobili (ICI)*. This is based on the offical value of the property – and those values may have been much lower than the actual values in the past, but are becoming much more realistic. The level is set by the local authority, and will be in the range of 0.4% to 0.7%.

Tax on rental income

If you have a rental income from your Italian property, then it is subject to tax.

- If you are a Italian resident, you will be subject to income tax. Currently the rates go from 23% on the first €16,000 up to 45% on income over €70,000, though there are allowances for dependants, medical bills, mortgage interest, life assurance and some other social costs. But there's a catch – your 'income' also includes a levy based on the rentable value of your house (whether it is rented or not). This is assessed locally and varies quite a lot, so talk to a local estate agent and find out what you may be facing before you commit.

- If you are a non-resident, the Italian taxman will take between 19% and 46% of any rental income, less repairs and other expenses (though not mortgage repayments). And what's left will be subject to UK income tax.

Lexicon: el investimento – investment

affitto (m)	rent
appartamento (m)	apartment
assicurazione (f)	insurance
caparra (f)	deposit
contratto (m) d'affitto	lease
imposta (f)	tax
imposta sugli immobili	property tax
imprenditore edile (m)	developer
interesse (m)	interest
investimento (m)	investment
IVA	VAT
mutuo (m)	mortgage
non ancora costruiti	off-plan
reddito (m)	income
rogito (m)	completion
seconda casa (f)	second home

English–Italian quick reference

apartment	appartamento (m)
completion	rogito (m)
deposit	caparra (f)
developer	imprenditore edile (m)

income	reddito (m)
insurance	assicurazione (f)
interest	interesse (m)
investment	investimento (m)
lease	contratto (m) d'affitto
mortgage	mutuo (m)
off-plan	non ancora costruiti
rent	affitto (m)
property tax	imposta sugli immobili
second home	seconda casa (f)
VAT	IVA – Imposta sul Valore Aggiunto

teach
yourself

italian
lydia vellaccio & maurice elston

- Do you want to cover the basics then progress fast?
- Have you got rusty Italian which needs brushing up?
- Do you want to reach a high standard?

Italian starts with the basics but moves at a lively pace to give
you a good level of understanding, speaking and writing. You will
have lots of opportunity to practise the kind of language you will
need to be able to communicate with confidence and understand
the culture of speakers of Italian.

teach
yourself

improve your italian
sylvia lymbery

- Have you got rusty Italian but don't want to start again?
- Do you want to get up to speed quickly?
- Are you looking for more than the simplest way of expressing yourself?

Improve your Italian is an ideal way to extend your language skills. You will build on your existing knowledge and improve your spoken and written Italian so that you can communicate with confidence in a range of situations, and at the same time you will learn about the country and its culture.

italian conversation
maria guarnieri & federica sturani

- Do you want to talk with confidence?
- Are you looking for basic conversation skills?
- Do you want to understand what people say to you?

Italian Conversation is a three-hour, all-audio course which
you can use at any time, whether you want a quick refresher
before a trip or whether you are a complete beginner. The 20
dialogues on CDs 1 and 2 will teach you the Italian you will
need to speak and understand, without getting bogged down
with grammar. CD 3, uniquely, teaches skills for listening and
understanding. This is the perfect accompaniment to
Beginner's Italian and **Italian** in the teach yourself range:
www.teachyourself.co.uk.

teach
yourself

italian vocabulary
mike zollo

- Do you want a quick way to increase your vocabulary?
- Are you looking for ways to help you remember new words?
- Do you want to improve your pronunciation?

Italian Vocabulary will build on what you already know to
increase your word power and give you confidence to speak.
The most important words have been identified for you, so you
won't waste time learning words you will never need.